Nurturing Babies

T0313025

Nurturing Babies explores the key processes behind how a child's mind and body develop in their first year, underpinned by the latest research in the fields of child development, psychology, health and well-being. It shows how the choices practitioners and parents make every day can have a deep impact on children's experiences and the practices that can be embedded straight away to support their ongoing development and give them the best opportunities for future success.

The book follows a holistic approach through the Nurturing Childhoods Pedagogical Framework, learning to understand children's evolving capabilities through their engagement in core behaviours and using these to unlock their full potential. Chapters cover:

- The importance of sleep and daily routines

- Playing and communicating with babies

- Physical activity and healthy eating

- Early brain development

- Understanding babies' emotions and behaviours

- The importance of emotional security on a child's well-being

- Supporting infants to explore and do new things

Part of the *Nurturing Childhoods* series, this exciting book provides practitioners and parents with the knowledge and understanding they need to nurture the very youngest children, building their self-esteem, happiness and well-being as they become enthusiastic lifelong learners.

Kathryn Peckham is a childhood consultant, researcher, author and founder of Nurturing Childhoods. She is an active member of global Early Childhood networks, conducting research for governments and international organisations, writing curricula and contributing to industry-leading publications and guidance such as Birth to 5 Matters.

Nurturing Babies

Developing the Potential of Every Child

Kathryn Peckham

Routledge
Taylor & Francis Group

LONDON AND NEW YORK

Designed cover image: © Getty Images

First edition published 2024
by Routledge
4 Park Square, Milton Park, Abingdon, Oxon, OX14 4RN

and by Routledge
605 Third Avenue, New York, NY 10158

Routledge is an imprint of the Taylor & Francis Group, an informa business

© 2024 Kathryn Peckham

The right of Kathryn Peckham to be identified as author of this work has been asserted in accordance with sections 77 and 78 of the Copyright, Designs and Patents Act 1988.

British Library Cataloguing-in-Publication Data
A catalogue record for this book is available from the British Library

ISBN: 978-1-032-35479-8 (hbk)
ISBN: 978-1-032-35478-1 (pbk)
ISBN: 978-1-003-32707-3 (ebk)

DOI: 10.4324/9781003327073

Typeset in Bembo
by SPi Technologies India Pvt Ltd (Straive)

Contents

Acknowledgements

It is with such great pleasure that I am able to share this series of books with you all. They have been many years in the creating and with numerous people to thank. Firstly, the staff and children at Olney Preschool and Olney Infant Academy in Buckinghamshire, England, the settings of the original research where I shared two years with the most delightful children and wonderfully accommodating and passionate staff.

I would also like to acknowledge the support of Bright Horizons Family Solutions UK, in providing images to illustrate the practice promoted in these publications. The Creative Services team at Bright Horizons worked collaboratively with me to supply the many delightful images of children and their carers engaging in playful and sensitive interactions. The images in these books were captured in various Bright Horizons nurseries throughout England and Scotland and with the kind permission of the parents to use these images of their fabulous children.

And I would like to thank my colleagues and friends at the Centre for Research in Early Childhood in Birmingham, most notably Professor Chris Pascal and Professor Tony Bertram, who listened tirelessly to my thoughts and ideas, helping me to unravel my excited sparks of inspiration into well-considered observations. A colleague once said to me that true creativity comes from the combination of knowledge, skill, inspiration and persistence, all of which were nurtured by this dynamic duo.

But as always, none of this would be possible without the ongoing love and support of my amazing husband and children who never stop believing in me. You have been there to read, to listen and on occasion to add some unique perspectives, all the while keeping me laughing... and fed! I could not do this without you.

Section I
Introduction

Nurturing childhoods for all our tomorrows

Children are amazing bundles of delight and possibility. Yep, even the overtired and hungry ones! They are full of emotions and expectations and they are driven to know and understand. From the moment they are born they are gathering all the experiences that their future learning, their relationships and their sense of self will be based upon. They then need environments that nurture their mind and body. They need opportunities to develop a sense of themselves and the world around them. They need to be stimulated, while feeling a sense of security and well-being, while at the same time experiencing an element of autonomy and control. They need to be seen and heard and for their well-being and happiness to be acknowledged and valued. And they need to be surrounded by adults who understand them and the nature of all this development.

Whether you are expecting your first child or been working in the industry for 30 years, you will have your own reasons for reading these books. But the fact that you are would suggest that you are well aware of the tremendous impact we all have on all the children in our lives through every decision we make, through every experience we facilitate and every interaction we share. And this starts now, during these amazing infant months when a baby is receiving their first experiences of the world and all it can offer.

It is then so important that we take the time to stop and think about what this means. What informs the way we interact? Are we aware of the experiences a baby needs … and doesn't need? How do we know if the environments we offer are purposeful and appropriate? Only when we think about these questions, rather than blindly going into each day hoping for the best, can we be consistent in our care and avoid being easily swayed by any number of different expectations, influences or unhelpful trends that are doing the rounds. Because the problem is, if you don't have a solid idea of your own values, you can end up going along with whatever comes your way. So, when you look into the eyes of an infant, knowing the impact you have in shaping their future, what

DOI: 10.4324/9781003327073-1

do you consider important? How do you know if it is right for this child in this moment? And how do you know the long-term impact you are having?

The books in the Nurturing Childhoods series will help you reflect on all that you do, whether you are an early years practitioner, a primary school teacher or a parent, whether you are experiencing your first child or in your 30th year. Our children are too important not to really understand what they need beyond a "one size fits all" curriculum, programme or approach. So, join me as we start looking beyond our adult agendas and look instead at the child in front of you as together we develop the potential of all our children.

Navigating your way around the series

There are four books in the series: *Nurturing Babies, Nurturing Toddlers; Nurturing Children through Preschool and Reception* and *Nurturing through the Primary Years* as illustrated in (Figure S1.1). Whilst these may sound similar to labels you associate with childcare and school establishments, each with its age boundaries and transitions, look again. You will find no age-related boundaries here. Whilst the way you care for and engage with a child will develop and mature, this is all about the child in front of you, rather than any arbitrary date on the calendar. Through these book titles we will focus our attentions on the needs and developments of preverbal children not yet able to freely navigate the world around them. We will look at toddlers who are getting to their feet and exploring more independently. We will then turn our attentions to children with a few more years' worth of experiences influencing all they do, before exploring the different realities faced by children as they enter more formal environments of learning.

Every child in your life is very much their own person, developing and learning through the experiences and influences that are central to their lives. Trying to group their needs, responses and outcomes is not only unhelpful, it also does our children a gross misservice and yet is something we can find ourselves trying to do as soon as we are confronted with boxes to place our children in. These books think of children in a very different way, bringing our focus back to the child rather than any adult-imposed criteria. This then avoids practices focused on a specific age range or outcome that can see us lose sight of the development that is occurring in the stages preceding it and those that follow, with areas the child needs to revisit or the areas in which they are racing ahead.

The books also acknowledge that children are on a lifelong journey of holistic, interconnected and continuously evolving development. To that end, many of the themes running through the books are relevant for all children and the intention is that you enjoy them all. For example, just because I introduce "Time for Rest" in this book does not mean that understanding a child's need to relax, what happens when they sleep and how we can introduce healthy restful habits is any less important as a child gets older. Communication, language and play are continual themes running through the books as we look at how they

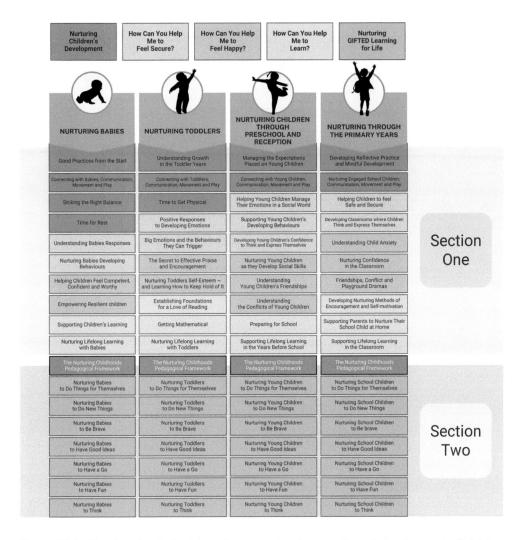

Nurturing Children's Development	How Can You Help Me to Feel Secure?	How Can You Help Me to Feel Happy?	How Can You Help Me to Learn?	Nurturing GIFTED Learning for Life
NURTURING BABIES	**NURTURING TODDLERS**	**NURTURING CHILDREN THROUGH PRESCHOOL AND RECEPTION**	**NURTURING THROUGH THE PRIMARY YEARS**	
Good Practices from the Start	Understanding Growth in the Toddler Years	Managing the Expectations Placed on Young Children	Developing Reflective Practice and Mindful Development	
Connecting with Babies; Communication, Movement and Play	Connecting with Toddlers; Communication, Movement and Play	Connecting with Young Children; Communication, Movement and Play	Nurturing Engaged School Children; Communication, Movement and Play	
Striking the Right Balance	Time to Get Physical	Helping Young Children Manage Their Emotions in a Social World	Helping Children to feel Safe and Secure	
Time for Rest	Positive Responses to Developing Emotions	Supporting Young Children's Developing Behaviours	Developing Classrooms where Children Think and Express Themselves	Section One
Understanding Babies Responses	Big Emotions and the Behaviours They Can Trigger	Developing Young Children's Confidence to Think and Express Themselves	Understanding Child Anxiety	
Nurturing Babies Developing Behaviours	The Secret to Effective Praise and Encouragement	Nurturing Young Children as they Develop Social Skills	Nurturing Confidence in the Classroom	
Helping Children Feel Competent, Confident and Worthy	Nurturing Toddlers Self-Esteem ~ and Learning How to Keep Hold of It	Understanding Young Children's Friendships	Friendships, Conflict and Playground Dramas	
Empowering Resilient children	Establishing Foundations for a Love of Reading	Understanding the Conflicts of Young Children	Developing Nurturing Methods of Encouragement and Self-motivation	
Supporting Children's Learning	Getting Mathematical	Preparing for School	Supporting Parents to Nurture Their School Child at Home	
Nurturing Lifelong Learning with Babies	Nurturing Lifelong Learning with Toddlers	Supporting Lifelong Learning in the Years Before School	Supporting Lifelong Learning in the Classroom	
The Nurturing Childhoods Pedagogical Framework	The Nurturing Childhoods Pedagogical Framework	The Nurturing Childhoods Pedagogical Framework	The Nurturing Childhoods Pedagogical Framework	
Nurturing Babies to Do Things for Themselves	Nurturing Toddlers to Do Things for Themselves	Nurturing Young Children to Do Things for Themselves	Nurturing School Children to Do Things for Themselves	
Nurturing Babies to Do New Things	Nurturing Toddlers to Do New Things	Nurturing Young Children to Do New Things	Nurturing School Children to Do New Things	
Nurturing Babies to Be Brave	Nurturing Toddlers to Be Brave	Nurturing Young Children to Be Brave	Nurturing School Children to Be brave	Section Two
Nurturing Babies to Have Good Ideas	Nurturing Toddlers to Have Good Ideas	Nurturing Young Children to Have Good Ideas	Nurturing School Children to Have Good Ideas	
Nurturing Babies to Have a Go	Nurturing Toddlers to Have a Go	Nurturing Young Children to Have a Go	Nurturing School Children to Have a Go	
Nurturing Babies to Have Fun	Nurturing Toddlers to Have Fun	Nurturing Young Children to Have Fun	Nurturing School Children to Have Fun	
Nurturing Babies to Think	Nurturing Toddlers to Think	Nurturing Young Children to Think	Nurturing School Children to Think	

Figure S1.1: The four books in this series, exploring the growth and development of children throughout their early childhood and on into the school classroom.

mature and develop, as is the development and understanding of a child's emotions and the behaviours they can trigger. And of course, the social skills I focus on in Nurturing Children through Preschool and Reception will already be embedding within them.

By its very nature, lifelong learning doesn't just apply to your children. We are all learning, through every word we read, image we see and moment we experience. Through these books I want you to learn something, but I won't achieve this by simply telling you what I think and expecting you to do the same. Every chapter is then written using the Nurturing Childhoods approach of *Knowledge, Understanding* and then *Support*. So, rather than looking to preach or dictate what I think you should do, the approach explains the reasons and puts those choices in your hands, the person with the child. And because of the preceding sections, you can really utilise all you are learning as you develop confident and consistent practice, ready to share with anyone.

Through an accessible style of writing and illustrations, each section can be easily and quickly understood, without the need for previous knowledge. So, whilst providing underpinning theory and new ways of thinking, these books are intended to be read and understood by anyone with an interest in young children as they help you think and reflect. What's more, because of their foundation in child development (rather than any curriculum) the relevance of these books will be maintained, regardless of changes in educational policy or documentation. This is also true wherever in the world you live, the programmes or policies that govern you, even the decade in which you read these words, because nurturing practice and understanding is both timeless and universal.

The books are also further supported by a setting-based accreditation and a suite of online courses for parents, practitioners and teachers. You can even join the Nurturing Childhoods Community, share your experiences and receive tons of support and guidance, so for more information, free workbooks and supplemental materials, head to nurturingchildhoods.com.

The learning child... yes – but what about the rest?

When a child is born they are already displaying some of the powerful tools of learning that have enabled us to thrive for hundreds of thousands of years. They are using social skills, eager to connect and find their place in this world. With curiosity they are stimulated through every interaction and experience, developing imaginations and playful techniques of learning. Every time we engage with a child, we are helping them develop these tools and their dispositions towards using them. Through the words we say, the tone we use and the body language we are perhaps not aware of, we are telling them more about how this world works. Is it worth them being curious, should they bother trying to socially engage, what happens when they try?

However, books written on the growth and development of children, both in their early years and in the school classroom, typically centre around the curriculums governing them and the learning goals and objectives that children are intended to work towards – essentially focusing on outcomes without looking at everything that informs them. As important as it is to keep a watchful eye on their development, alert to any concerns that may need some extra support, a child is more than a product of their development goals, all of which will be greatly influenced by the world around them. We cannot nurture a child's development until we have explored the wider implications of what it means to be a child in that moment. You would question an aircraft designer whose only way of knowing the validity of their designs was through flight trials before knowing the aerodynamics of the craft, the security of every nut and bolt or whether a storm is brewing. How secure would you feel getting on board?

We do then need to know our children, from the inside out. We need to nurture these characteristics developing through every experience and we need to observe and really see, without the blinkers of outcome expectations. Only then can we encourage their love of knowing and understanding, helping them to recognise the power that resides within them, and with an informed glance, learn so much more about the journey they are on than any curriculum or development guide can begin to tell us. I will then introduce you to the concept of GIFTED Learning, or the Greater Involvement Facilitated Through Engaging in Dispositions. GIFTED Learning recognises that we are facilitating children's earliest experiences of the learning process through everything we do, nurturing them as they experience what it means to be curious, to make independent choices and to think for themselves.

We also know the importance of a child's well-being and involvement from the work of many esteemed colleagues in the field. The idea of there being a hierarchy of needs is also nothing new and yet, if curriculum driven, we can find ourselves overly concerned with outcomes without considering the full impact that we ourselves are having on them. The learning child is important yes, but a small part of everything a child represents and yet a greater level of understanding can be missing from many childcare qualifications and subsequently a lot of practice. And yet meaningful learning simply isn't possible if a child does not feel safe and secure in their surroundings. Unless we learn to see children in a more holistic way, the whole set-up is prone to topple as illustrated in Figure S1.2 below.

These books take a very different approach to what you may have read before. Instead of focusing on learning goals or developmental milestones, we take a look at the holistic nature of a child, rooted in their need for engagement, movement and play. We will look at what it means for a child to feel secure, understanding how their behaviours reflect their sense of safety and well-being. And we will look at how our environments, engagements and every decision we make feed into a child's sense of agency and the factors that go a long way to determining their happiness.

In Section 1 you will find chapters that look at how we nurture children's development, how we can help children to feel secure, how we can help them find their happiness and then how we can nurture their love of learning and enquiry. All while offering the experiences and underpinning features that are important to learning and the dispositions of an enthusiastic lifelong learner.

In Section 2 I will introduce you to a new way of thinking about children's development and the way you observe and facilitate it, whether you are working in the UK, the USA or the UAE; whether you follow a Montessori, High Scope or Forest School Approach; whether you care for children in a huge centre, a forest or your spare room as parents, practitioners, teachers or family support workers. This starts by keeping CHILDREN at the centre of all we do and recognising that they have been doing a very good job of growing and developing for hundreds of thousands of years. We just need to know how to look and really see them, rather than tie ourselves up in the knots of external agendas that can change at any moment.

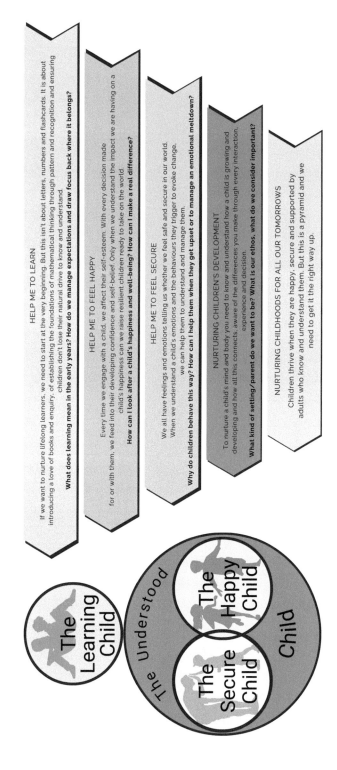

Nurturing The Whole Child:

Happy, Secure and Ready to Take on the World

HELP ME TO LEARN

If we want to nurture lifelong learners, we need to start at the very beginning. But this isn't about letters, numbers and flashcards. It is about introducing a love of books and enquiry, of establishing the foundations of mathematical thinking through pattern and recognition and ensuring children don't lose their natural drive to know and understand.

What does learning mean in the early years? How do we manage expectations and draw focus back where it belongs?

HELP ME TO FEEL HAPPY

Every time we engage with a child, we affect their self-esteem. With every decision made for or with them, we feed into their developing confidence and self-belief. Only when we understand the impact we are having on a child's happiness can we raise resilient children ready to take on the world.

How can I look after a child's happiness and well-being? How can I make a real difference?

HELP ME TO FEEL SECURE

We all have feelings and emotions telling us whether we feel safe and secure in our world. When we understand a child's emotions and the behaviours they trigger to evoke change, we can help them to understand and manage them.

Why do children behave this way? How can I help them when they get upset or to manage an emotional meltdown?

NURTURING CHILDREN'S DEVELOPMENT

To nurture a child's mind and body you need to know and understand how a child is growing and developing and how all this connects, aware of the differences you make through every interaction, experience and decision.

What kind of setting/parent do we want to be? What is our ethos, what do we consider important?

NURTURING CHILDHOODS FOR ALL OUR TOMORROWS

Children thrive when they are happy, secure and supported by adults who know and understand them. But this is a pyramid and we need to get it the right way up.

The Learning Child

The Understood Child

The Secure Child

The Happy Child

Figure S1.2: Developing the learning skills and capabilities of a child might be at the top of our agenda, but it rests on so much more that we need to get right first.

This is then about embracing a child's holistic, continual and constantly evolving development, recognising that it is embedded within the environment, engagements and permissions in which it is situated and that it is deeply impacted by a child's sense of happiness and security in the moment. All of this will be reflected in the levels of engagement that are possible, if only we focus our attentions on the behaviours and responses of the child. Because when we can do that, children flourish in the ways they have been instinctively trying to do for millennia. They can do so as babies, toddlers… and all the way through the school system in ways that protect them from changing directives, unknown futures and the realities of a universally connected world. To that end, I will then introduce you to the Nurturing Childhoods Pedagogical Framework (NCPF)… aka, The Flower.

While this may at first seem a little more complex than a development framework you are familiar with, child development is far more deep-rooted than fitting children into neat descriptions. They cannot demonstrate all you need to know through an activity designed to meet today's learning goals. But they speak volumes through every behaviour and response, provided you know how to see them. If you want to capture this level of understanding of the children in your life, not only do you need to be led by the child in front of you, but you also need methods that will allow for deeper reflection and a more informed awareness of the experiences you offer. By the time you have finished reading this series, you will then have all of that too.

Navigating your way around this book

In Section 1 of this book we will reflect on why the decisions you make for children have such a big impact on their future development, the importance of every experience and the key practices that make all the difference (Figure S1.3). We will look at how impactful their early environments are and how important this is for their emotional stability. We will think about how children engage and connect during these first months and the impact you have on these processes through every interaction as you engage and play. We will consider how the brain is wiring up and the opportunities babies need for deep-rooted physical and cognitive development. And we will explore what happens to their bodies and minds when they sleep, how much sleep children need at different times in their lives and the importance of establishing routines, mindful of sleep cycles.

As we look at helping babies to feel secure, we will examine how we experience our emotions and the ways they affect children and their sense of security. We will consider the processes going on inside when strong emotions are experienced and how we can help babies manage stressful moments. As we discover ways of supporting the early stages of emotional intelligence, we will also note what happens when these are not effectively managed. We will look at how behaviours develop and the effects

Chapters exploring the importance of nurturing children's holistic development

NURTURING CHILDREN IN THE EARLY YEARS

As we explore how children's minds and bodies are growing in the early years we will consider the magnitude of impact and the differences you make every time you talk to a baby, listen to a toddler or engage in a hunt for spiders with older children. We will look at the expectations placed on children and those caring for them and refocus our attention where it is really important. We will look at what happens when you play with a child, making eye contact and engaging, as well as provide lots of practical advice and guidance.

HOW CAN YOU HELP ME TO FEEL SECURE?

These chapters will help you look at children's developing emotions and behaviours. We consider how we can help children to understand their emotions, how we can support them to express themselves and make friends and, as the child matures, how to manage more difficult behaviours, supporting children to feel safe and secure, able to express themselves and make friends, even when experiencing the tough emotions that we can all experience.

HOW CAN YOU HELP ME TO FEEL HAPPY?

Whilst we can't make a child feel happy, or feel any emotion for that matter, we can help them to develop their confidence, their self-esteem and resilience. We can support them as they find their place in this social world, able to make friends, express their needs and feel capable of achieving that which would make them happy, all with a growth mindset that sees them take life's setbacks with an air of optimism rather than defeat.

HOW CAN YOU HELP ME TO LEARN?

These chapters look at supporting our children's learning from day one. But rather than letters, numbers and flashcards and a programme of activities, we look instead at the practices we can introduce to support a love of books and enquiry, of establishing the foundations of mathematical thinking through pattern, observation and purpose and ensuring children don't lose the natural drive to know and understand that they are born with. All of this begins from the tiniest babies and continues into the primary years.

NURTURING GIFTED LEARNING FOR LIFE

In Section 2 we will explore the Nurturing Childhoods Pedagogical Framework (NCPF) as a new way to understand and nurture a GIFTED Learning approach. Keeping children very much at the centre of all we do, the NCPF recognises the Greater Involvement we can Facilitate when children Engage in their Dispositions and we will explore this through seven critical behaviours in line with the growing capabilities of the child in focus. It will look at why this is so important, their impact on future attitudes towards learning and how this can all be nurtured from day one.

Figure S1.3: Through these we will explore the importance of nurturing children holistically throughout their early childhood and the primary years.

we have on this process when we respond to a baby in different ways, mindful of their need to feel secure. We consider how this drives a child's behaviours and how you can help manage their triggers by reflecting on the influences and environments you are offering.

As we look at helping babies to feel happy, we will consider what this means and the foundations of happiness that begin embedding during early childhood. We will discuss practices that promote self-esteem and well-being, along with the importance of resilience and its underpinning characteristics. And we will examine how a child's experiences deeply impact these ongoing processes.

As we contemplate ways of helping babies to learn, we will start by exploring the difference between learning and teaching a child. We will then look at how children learn in the first years of life, the factors this depends on and the importance of every moment. We will then reflect on how we harness engagement and embed the foundations of learning through the experiences children receive from day one, helping all the key adults in their life to do the same.

In Section 2 we will take this holistic approach further as we explore the Nurturing Childhoods Pedagogical Framework (NCPF). Through the series we will explore the framework at progressively deeper levels as the abilities and capabilities of children become more complex. Then in the final chapters, we will learn to really see everything that our infants are communicating to us through their behaviours and the powerful ways we have to nurture their full potential. Through this approach, we can learn to use the NCPF lens to re-evaluate the choices we extend to our children, the opportunities these choices offer for them to think for themselves, to be curious and to want to try their ideas and socially engage.

Igniting the potential of dispositional development

If you have spent any time in the company of a child you will know that their experiences never occur in a vacuum. You will have seen how processes of learning and development are dynamic, fluid and influenced by a myriad of unique variables specific to each child and the moment you are sharing. And yet in a landscape where recognised progress often hinges on a child's demonstrated abilities within predefined developmental milestones, many foundational experiences are being overlooked and the powerful dispositions our children are born with are being devalued.

Imagine instead if a dispositional focus rooted in the theories and methods offered here were to accompany development goals. Think what could be possible if every child's natural instincts for learning were recognised and developed throughout their childhood, wherever they may reside. What could be possible if every child could maintain the same level of motivation in learning to read as they had when learning to walk, if every time they stumbled over a new challenge they simply picked themselves up and tried again. But to do this children need ongoing experiences that cultivate their courage, persistence and a belief in their own potential for success. They need to retain the imagination and curiosity that drove their explorations as a baby, whilst experiencing the power that comes from their own efforts.

While it's inevitable that a child's opportunities will be largely guided by adults throughout the day, if we limit the richness of these experiences to mere external agendas, developmental objectives or acquired skills, we significantly curtail their potential for growth in ways that also reverberate throughout their emotional and social wellbeing. Instead we must look to preserve all children's innate behaviours, encouraging their natural curiosity and inclinations to engage. This means granting children a voice, agency and opportunities for independent thought, supported by advocates who champion every child's right to ponder, to question and to imagine as they demonstrate their full range of capabilities, not just to an onlooker, but to themselves.

The methods you will gain through reading the Nurturing Childhoods series are all underpinned by a longitudinal phenomenological study and decades of research, providing you with a comprehensive and holistic framework for understanding your children's development (Peckham, 2021). These insights can be seamlessly integrated with any curriculum, program or approach, allowing you to consider the impact of your actions and interactions, your environments and pedagogies, both formal and informal. This empowers you to not only capture the intricate constructs inherent in learning and development, but also the social and cultural dynamics that shape children's experiences and the ultimate outcomes they will attain. The book series recognises the profound influence that pedagogical choices wield on a child's depth of engagement and their evolving attitudes towards learning, both in the moment and as their predispositions take root. So, as you embark on the journey of nurturing your children during their early years, I hope this book encourages you to re-evaluate the experiences you are offering, mindful of their deeper potential as you tap into these fundamental human instincts that have propelled us all towards staggering levels of learning from our first days of life.

Reference

Peckham, K. (2021) A phenomenological study exploring how early childhood pedagogies enable the development of dispositions. Doctoral thesis, Birmingham City University.

Good practices from the start

From your first interaction with a child the processes of attachment are already beginning. Whether this is at the moment of their birth as they are placed in your arms or some months later as you meet them for the first time. As you make contact, pleasure receptors are lighting up in their brain as they seek to make connections with you. As they make eye contact, inviting you to engage, you find yourself smiling warmly and slipping into the melodic way we tend to engage with very young children.

As social beings we are driven to connect in these ways, automatically finding ourselves responding to the people around us. But for young children who are otherwise defenceless, these mechanisms are ensuring their survival. And the fact that you managed to ensure your survival for long enough to read these words today suggests that you yourself did a pretty good job of it. But you did so much more besides.

You were able to secure sufficient nutrition for yourself to survive and flourish, you managed to find the protection that allowed you to rest in safety and the warmth and security to make it through thousands of days and nights. You were considered valuable enough to educate, to treat when you became unwell. And you were given the opportunities and experiences to have fostered enough of an interest in the world around you to learn and perfect a multitude of skills. To talk and make yourself understood, to read someone else's words and understand the thoughts of the person who wrote them, to know the foods you like and the pastimes you enjoy. Every experience you have had in your life has led to this moment, equipping you with the skills you need and forming the person you have become.

DOI: 10.4324/9781003327073-2

If you have young children in your life, you are in the amazing position of being instrumental in this process for someone else. Every decision you make and action you take impacts this process from day one. But no two children are the same, nor any two days with them. And they certainly don't come with a personalised user guide. Despite this, well-intentioned advice will be coming at you from every angle, and it can be difficult to know who to turn to for trusted guidance as you make the decisions that will have such a profound impact on the next generation (Figure 1.1).

Figure 1.1: The impact we have on the children in our lives is monumental. Through every engagement, interaction and decision we make on their behalf.

Knowledge

Know why the decisions you make for children have such a big impact on future development

There really is no more important job than how we care for the youngest members of our society, but then I might be biased. Whether you are caring for your own child or working as part of a team in a busy setting, your approach and the underpinning theories that guide you are then of great importance, whether you know what these are called or where they originated.

However, all this can seem like quite an awesome responsibility. If you have ever met a child, you will realise that in the heat of the moment they are unlikely to offer you the time you need to carefully consider how you would like to act. Instead, you may find yourself needing to respond very quickly and, potentially, when you are not in the best place to do so. Pushed for time, short on resources or facing a room full of hungry tummies, you will rarely have the luxury or the peace and quiet to simply stop and think.

So, where do you go for trusted guidance?

Everyone, it seems, is eager to offer suggestions when it comes to caring for children. From the anecdotal advice you hear over a coffee, to any one of a hundred sites you may land on when looking to the internet for advice. Some may be based in scientific research, others far less so. And the truth is, while you may be surrounded by these influences, it is your opinions, beliefs and actions that are going to count in the moment. And these will be informed by a mix of all these things and more, resulting in the personal set of styles and techniques, methods and practices that you employ.

When it comes to childcare and early experiences of education, you may be aware of many pedagogical approaches. These may look at the curriculum, or the content of what is being taught, the methods by which it is delivered or the learning theories that underpin it. In some countries the early childcare and education (ECEC) offered to young children is integrated and governed by a common curriculum. In other countries, a more diverse approach is used, chosen to respond to the different societal needs and communities where they are delivered. This may be centred around a given learning environment or a belief in the holistic learning needs of young children. It may be driven through intentional teaching or learning through play. All of which could be underpinned by constructivist, behaviourist or experiential learning theories. All have the intention of enabling learning to take place with opportunities for children to gain the knowledge, skills, attitudes and dispositions that are considered to be important.

This then immediately asks the question… what do YOU consider to be important?

While it is true that no two children are the same, the fundamental processes of growth and development that guide them are. So, it is only natural to look for support and insights wherever we can. But how do you begin to understand what children need? You may have seen practice in other countries, read books or seen pictures of amazing environments and fallen in love with the pedagogies being demonstrated or the approaches being described. However, any curricula or educational philosophy you view will be underpinned by a set of methods, techniques and learning theories that you need to be aware of. These will be influenced by the positionality of its authors and possibly the agendas of those embracing it.

Wherever the underpinning research originated, it will have been carried out by considering the growth and development of children through a certain theoretical perspective, like a lens that observations are viewed and interpreted through. It may be based on theories developed long ago, with children living or learning in very different circumstances than the children you see every day. It could have been structured to nurture children within a culture or landscape very different to your own. And whilst these considerations do not prevent children everywhere from thriving within them, we do need to be mindful of them before adopting the theories and practices of others wholesale.

Whether you can select the style and method of practice that suits you or you are expected to follow the approach of those you work with, it is important that you understand the pedagogical theory behind the styles of practice you follow and the experiences children receive when your practice is informed by them. It is then important that you consider:

- Where did this advice come from?

- Who wrote it or said it and what makes them an authority on the subject?

- What agenda is behind it?

- What evidence or research supports it?

- How does this fit with my own ethos, understanding and values?

- Is this something I want to follow?

Without this mental checklist, we can find ourselves blindly following every latest fad or trending technique, making decisions based on someone else's changing motives or agendas. Or see costly purchases fuelled by the carefully worded messages of a commercial marketing team. Whatever decisions you make, your children need you to follow them with consistency and confidence. To do this, you need to have a good understanding of your own knowledge along with the framework or pedagogical approach that you will apply it through.

Why is this so important?

The child development theories used to underpin your pedagogy, your curriculum or the ethos you work within will impact all you do. It will determine the outcomes you consider to be important and guide the environments and resources you offer and most importantly, the experiences children gain when they are with you. With a carefully considered pedagogical approach, you will have this structure in place to guide you. But care must be taken that you understand the core principles that it is based on. And that it is rooted in a contemporary understanding of child development (Figure 1.2).

Figure 1.2: Everything you do when caring for a child will be impacted by your personal theories and knowledge of what you consider to be important. This does then require some thought.

With every experience in a young child's life informing the way they respond to the next one, these decisions are affecting a child's development in a profound way – and ultimately the person this child will become. A child's early years are, then, a uniquely special time; foundational to all future growth and development and yet experienced within such a short period of time, every moment of which must be valued and cherished for the opportunities, potential and magical moments they hold.

When you have a clear understanding of the thinking behind a given practice and you are able to combine this with the child development knowledge you need to effectively implement it, its intentions can be realised. But this is only half the process. To know whether this is working for you and the children in your care, you also need to implement effective processes of reflection. Only then can you remain mindful of your intentions and whether these are being met through your actions.

When you have the knowledge and understanding of how children develop, you can begin to trust in your own instincts. Once you know how their brain and body are maturing and understand the complex processes that are occurring, you can begin to rely on your own science, developing techniques that work for you, your families and your setting; trusting in your instincts as you respond to the unique child you are with, informed through their actions and behaviours as you take advantage of all the opportunities around you and discerning the techniques you do want to follow, from the methods that never did quite sit comfortably, regardless of what you may have read or who else may seem convinced by them.

And in all things, continue to ask yourself, "Why am I doing this?" If you find yourself answering with anything other than "Because it's the best thing for the *child*", take a moment to think again.

Understanding

Understand how impactful early environments, engagements and routines are to babies

Environments where babies can feel nurtured

Let me start by asking you what you think of when picturing a child's nursery. What colours are you seeing, what sounds can you hear and what play resources are filling it? Is the environment segmented or free-flowing? Who else is in the environment? Is it busy or calm, peaceful or vibrant? Depending on your own experiences and expectations, your answers to these questions may be quite different to a colleague's. You may find yourself having quite an emotional reaction, ranging from a serene smile of delight to abject terror, perhaps prompted through visions of overly bright and noisy environments, simultaneously competing to invigorate your senses and demand your attention.

When considering the nurturing environments we offer to babies, it is important to consider their needs, how they learn and how this experience feels to them. Where are their personal needs being taken care of? Are there opportunities for shared moments of calm during a feed or to make the connections that allow for deep attachments to develop? And how are their senses being engaged and stimulated without being overwhelmed?

I closed the last section by asking you to consider "Why am I doing this?" and this is a technique we can usefully apply here. If you are beginning to set up a new environment for a baby or looking to observe an established one through a different lens, ask yourself this question as you consider each element. Reminding yourself as you do so that, while we do all learn through the experiences we receive and the senses these experiences stimulate, in this instance there absolutely is such a thing as having too much of a good thing.

In Chapter 3 we will explore how children learn through their senses, but to do so they need considered opportunities. How can they fine-tune their hearing in an environment that is filled with competing noise? How can they touch, explore and investigate with their whole bodies in an environment where it is not safe or permitted for them to do so? Of the items that have been purchased, who they have been designed to appeal to? And if you are not sure, how many times has a child been compelled to engage with or notice them?

No toy or resource is as valuable as the time, engagement and understanding that you can offer to a child. Despite this, every manufacturer, glossy magazine or social media post would have you believe otherwise. More than any of these commercial purchases, babies need to feel protected and safe. They need adults around them who understand the importance of their early years and they need to feel loved and securely attached.

They do need stimulation, but they also need opportunities to see and hear the things around them without becoming overwhelmed. They need opportunities to try things for themselves, to feel how their bodies work and the responses they can generate. And they need space to rest at a moment's notice. Only once a child feels secure within a stable and safe environment can their attention then turn to other things (Figure 1.3).

Figure 1.3: Babies need stimulation, but they also need a calm environment where they can rest when they need to.

The importance of engagement and interactions

Growing more rapidly in mind and body during these first years than at any other time of the child's life, we must be mindful of the importance of our interactions and what they offer. Our children are so interested in everything around them because they are learning all about the diverse and boggling world they live in, as well as their place within it. They are seeking to understand how their body works, what they can do with it and how they can use it to encourage a range of reactions from others.

But it is so much more than this. During these foundational years of a child's life, they are also formulating the tastes, habits and beliefs that will become entrenched into their thinking and behaviours long into the future, establishing the person they will become, as well as the tastes, habits and beliefs they will hand down to future genera-tions. Like with many influences in a child's life, these originate within the choices being made even long before a baby is even born.

Every moment of these precious first years should then be cherished and seen for the gifts that you can offer a child. That does not mean filling a space with every resource, but thinking carefully about the resources you offer. It doesn't mean feeling guilty about the jobs you need to be doing, but it does mean connecting with children when you are with them, making eye contact, taking the time to focus your attention on their interests and engaging with them. This is just as important as you carry out all the care routines of the day as it is during times of play.

We are all social creatures and, in these moments, the social bonds and attachments vital to all future relationships and learning are being secured. These engagements and interactions are also telling that child how much they are valued; how worthy of your time and attention they are and that their interests are worth pursuing. Only when these are in place can any deep-rooted learning and development occur.

Routines and structure or child led and flow

You will find that, with many aspects of caring for young children, there are polar opposite ideas of what children need and the approaches that should be followed. Typically the best response tends to be "somewhere in the middle". When it comes to routines and structure, very young children are indeed seeking to establish a sense of security and stability around them. They are remarkably aware that they are defenceless and relying on others to supply everything they need. And when this seems to be taking a little longer than expected or is different than before, their sense of security can become threatened, with a resulting fallout that can be easily imagined. Routines and structure within their day can help with this, as can common and repeated actions such as getting a bib from the same drawer before a feed or gentle music on the lead-up to sleep time. Humans are remarkably good at spotting patterns within our experiences and these approaches can help children to know what is to come next and to manage their expectations of it.

That said, life doesn't always run on a schedule. Sometimes unexpected events can happen, causing delays or offering unplanned opportunities. It is so important at this early stage to introduce babies to these diverse experiences, developing the enjoyment, taste and acceptance of a wide range of activities, environments and people that their later learning, health and relationships are relying on.

Children at any age can also become absorbed in what they are doing and every care should be taken not to destroy these moments because the clock suggests it is time for the next item on your agenda. Have a structure in mind, but observe a child before swooping in. Understand the signs that suggest they have had enough of something before taking them away. And respect their growing awareness of what they need, rather than assuming you know what a child wants in this moment more than they do. A baby will soon show you with a turn of the head or a fractious grumble that this activity is no longer absorbing. But all the time it is holding their attention, the feed or change can wait a moment.

Then, when you are ready to move on, offer them the cues they need to start mapping the flow of events in their own mind. As they develop the skills they need to ready themselves for change, they will become less surprised by it. When they regularly see you get out their hat and coat, they begin to associate this with going outside. Hearing you lay the table or warm a bottle means a feed is on its way. Whereas sitting quietly sharing a book together might mean we are getting ready for sleep.

Support

Be supported to consider the routines, objectives and expectations at the centre of all you do

As you look to consider how you care for and support the growth and development of young babies, begin again by bringing the child back to the centre of all you do. And as you question any of your practices, think of the nature of what it is you are doing and who you are doing it for. As I said, unless the root of this response is "Because it's the best thing for the <u>child</u>", you may like to re-examine what your motivations are.

Sometimes the needs and objectives of others may need to be accommodated. There may be older children who must arrive at school on time, a meal you need to start preparing or a room full of babies with competing needs that must all be considered. But if your responses are more along the lines of "The expectation is that I will do it this way", I hadn't really thought about it" or "This is the way it has always been done", you need to question what is driving your practice.

Get to know the child in front of you today

The only way you can know if you are following the practices your children need from you is to take the time to get to know them – free of the expectations of what you might like them to be doing or saying. This might seem like an odd thing to say, but it is amazing how many practices are done automatically without much thought, when our children are unique and changing every day (Figure 1.4).

Figure 1.4: Take the time to get to know each child in this moment, as you resist falling into automatic practices.

Watch their behaviours and tendencies as they interact and engage with their world. As you begin to really see them and their developments day by day, you can observe their actions and responses on a different level. Recognise their behaviours for what they are telling you. How do they gain the attention of those around them? How do they show you they are tired, hungry or in need of different stimulation? What practices soothe them in these moments and which simply frustrate? If you are part of a busy setting, establish methods of sharing this knowledge with each other, developing the benefits of shared experiences and reflective practice. And if you are doing it alone, join many of the shared networks of practice that are available to you, such as the community you can join at the *Nurturing Childhoods Academy* (academy.nurturing childhoods. co.uk) as you benefit from shared experiences and gain an informed understanding.

Once you begin to focus on your own children, who you know better than anyone, this will offer you more insight than any "How To" guide or internet search can begin to. And as your understanding of how children grow and develop builds, so too will your awareness of their responses and the meaning of them as you learn to view their behaviours not as effectively designed to try your patience but as core milestones on a child's way to becoming resilient, courageous and empathetic young adults.

Take the time to observe what they are doing and the ways they are doing it. Once you learn to trust in your informed instincts you will begin to feel like your very own "Baby Whisperer" as you begin to know what is right for your children and your families. And when you learn to look without a predetermined intention or an agenda to follow, you are ready to question any established "knowledge" you may read or advice you may hear with the confidence to take a moment, reflect on your child's needs and if necessary, challenge it.

Establishing nurturing environments

When looking to establish a nurturing environment for babies, it is often tempting to think about colour schemes, must-have resources and pictures of nurseries we have seen and liked. The trouble with this approach is that rarely are any of these things designed with the child at their centre. While the best environments will be as diverse as the number of people reading these words, the factors used to direct them will be universal. So, consider these factors as you think about the environments, experiences and opportunities you offer to the youngest children in your care.

Firstly, look to create a sense of safety and security. If you are looking to establish an environment where a very young child may be spending a good deal of time during these early months, think about all the growth and development that is occurring during the time they will be with you and how responsible for it you will be. None of this is possible if the child's primary sense of safety and security is out of balance. How ready do you feel to do anything if you are not sure where you are, who may be there or what might happen next? Now imagine this without the words or independence to do anything about it.

■ Is the environment calm and soothing? While children learn through their senses, becoming overly stimulated is not a pleasurable state to be in.

■ Can a baby experience the warmth, rest and attention they need when they need it? For a young infant whose body and mind needs to regularly switch off, this is an important consideration.

■ Are levels of stress being managed within the environment? Young babies will have an emotionally charged reaction whenever an experience becomes too stressful for them to manage effectively.

■ Is there a sense of emotional stability, love and security in an environment kept free from excessively negative experiences… and mindful of what these might be?

■ How are children spoken to and engaged with? Don't just assume, consciously monitor it. How often does someone look into their eyes and really connect?

■ Are there moments throughout the day to engage over food or a story?

■ Is the environment reflective of just how engaged a young brain is? Does it respect a child's powerful drives to explore and understand?

■ Where do care routines happen? Are they warm and nurturing, away from hustle and bustle so that the child can feel relaxed during these intimate moments?

When you begin to understand how a young brain and body is developing, the importance of every moment during these short few years can be realised. We can consider ways of facilitating opportunities for a child who is dependent on others for everything along with the impact of every meaningfully gained experience, as they investigate and explore their environment, captivated by the result of their actions.

As they learn through their senses, consider how these are being stimulated.

■ What can they see, hear, smell, taste and touch? Remembering that often, less is more!

■ Can they detect subtle differences in sound, tone and rhythm? A child learning about their world through the sounds they can hear needs to distinguish these subtle changes.

■ Are you selective about when you use music? Do you think about the colours and colourful objects you introduce or the range of materials they can touch and explore?

If you want to really understand what your environment is like for a baby, you need to remind yourself of what it feels like to be one. Get down on the floor, what can you see? Crawl around on your hands and knees, how does that feel? Imagine where you would like to go, how are you going to get there? And how will you engage with others if they are all now towering above you?

It is my belief, after many years of working with children and families and of studying the intricacies of childhood development, growth and behaviour, that once armed with an informed understanding, you are in a much better position to recognise and interpret the needs of children. Only then can you distinguish between their demands, emotions and behaviours and be in a secure position to support and manage them.

Children take all of childhood to grow; there are no quick fixes. Brains are developing, bodies are growing, and the world is a confusing place that your children are only beginning to navigate their way around. So, enjoy this time as you support their well-being and your own as you guide them through this tremendous period of rapid growth and development, aware of who they are, where they have come from and what they need to be ready for next. And most importantly, enjoy them in the here and now, rather than expecting the more mature responses of the child they are yet to become.

2 Connecting with babies
Communication, movement and play

Through the connections a child receives and the opportunities they are given to engage, a child is establishing an understanding of how this social world works. And through the responses they receive, they are developing a sense of their importance in the eyes of those around them as their self-esteem and personal identity take root. This is important at every age, as we keep these vital paths of communication open, but it begins with the tiniest of babies and the enriched opportunities you can offer from day one.

How you communicate with children, from the body language you display and the facial expressions you greet them with to how you hold them, the tone of your voice and the eye contact you make are all sending signals to your infant, telling them that they are loved and valued. Every positive experience with a child reinforces these messages of love, security, and emotional attachment, allowing them to feel reassured. Firstly, of your presence and then of your understanding and support. As you take care of their needs you send them the message that they are worth caring about as a secure relationship flourishes. And with each subsequent positive action, a sense of stability and well-being is established and developed within them, informing all their future interactions.

That said, you won't always get it right and mistakes will be made now and in all the years to come. Whether they are trying to tell you that they are hungry when you are struggling to put them down for a nap; frustrated over putting their own shoes on when you are trying to get out the door; or distraught over an insensitive comment from a friend that you failed to appreciate – in all these moments, children are relying on the sensitive communication skills that are embedding from the beginning.

By developing the skills needed to connect through communication, movement and play you can support a child's emotional well-being, ready for all the trials and tribulations that the coming years will offer. By showing them that the adults around them do listen and really hear what they have to say, you can effectively support their sense of belonging and establish within them a secure sense of self.

DOI: 10.4324/9781003327073-3

Knowledge

Know how children's abilities to connect are growing and developing in these first months

A baby will have been listening to voices and conversations since their time in the womb; a noisy place with low level sounds travelling well through their fluid environment. Once they are born even tiny babies have been shown to have a strong preference for human voices over other noises, as they look to communicate and play. Turning their heads towards human voices more often than any non-speech sound, this is especially true of the higher pitched, sing-song pattern of child-directed speech we can naturally slip into when speaking to a young infant as we are drawn into their attempts to make eye contact and engage (Figure 2.1).

Figure 2.1: Every time we look into the eyes of an infant, deep connections are being made.

Communication

The style of communication we tend to slip into when speaking to an infant is known as motherese and is used the world over. Accentuating the tones babies need to hear to recognise and develop speech, we slow down our words and accentuate our vowels, naturally changing our pitch and tone at the start and finish of our sentences. These techniques make it easier for young children to hear the rhythm of language long before any real meaning is absorbed from the words you are saying. Research has shown that babies prefer this style and actually learn more from it.

But when engaging with a young child, remember: they can understand far more than they can say. So, while you happily engage in a motherese style of speech and normal speech, be mindful that they are continuously learning from you. Talk to them in the same ways that you would talk to an older child, using long, complex sentences of interest to them, to you and of the day with lots of different words. In these moments, children are learning all about the tone and cadence of your language long before any real meaning is absorbed from the words you are saying.

Making a variety of vocal sounds from the moment they are born, children are developing the skills and techniques of communicating through language. At around four to ten months they will begin repeating sounds back to you that include both a consonant and a vowel. These sounds are recognisable as the syllables within speech, for example "ma ma ma" or "be be be". This precursor to speech is called canonical babbling and is a babies' way of practising the pronunciation of syllables, the building blocks of complete words. Saying their first words really comes when a child can connect a meaning to the sounds they are making and this can happen from six months when, unsurprisingly, the words they hear used in conversation with them every day are the ones they recognise with the most success.

However, like with all children's developmental milestones, it is normal for the timing of speech milestones to fluctuate. That said, there are guidelines in place to help you identify when a little extra support may be required so that early delays do not become limiting factors in other developmental areas. But with some studies suggesting that approximately 25% of children have not spoken their first words by the age of 12 months, when should you worry? If a child has not started canonical babbling by the time they are around nine months old, monitor this and talk to your health-care professional for some advice. You can expect their first words typically between 11–13 months, with major improvements in their understanding of speech by around 14 months. If this is not your experience, again consult with your health-care professional. With a little additional support in these early days, many of the potential issues a child may otherwise face can be eased or resolved. However, the longer communication issues are left, the more likely a child is to experience the range of problems that can be associated with them.

Movement

In these earliest weeks and months, a baby's mind and body is growing at a rapid rate. Imagine how it must feel if every morning you woke up to find your body was not quite as you left it the day before. To keep pace with these changes, children need to constantly use their bodies, feeling where things are and how they connect. This goes some way to explaining why they are constantly moving, flailing their arms and legs, exploring their hands and feet as they adapt their receptors to accommodate today's version of "me". This is also why they can become increasingly upset when left in any position for too long or denied these opportunities to move.

When children are given opportunities to explore their environment, they are developing all the muscles and systems in the body – even those you might not immediately think of. The muscles deep within a baby's eyes need experiences of looking to the near and far distance. Their vestibular system, responsible for balance, muscle tone and bilateral coordination, needs stimulating and strengthening through their movements and their changes in position. Sat in one position, looking at the toys placed at the same distance around them, cannot adequately stimulate these systems, so instead, encourage them to stretch, reach and use their bodies to investigate the world around them. Offer them lots of experiences that inspire them to touch and manipulate, to see what happens if and to see whether they can.

A hugely important experience for your developing infants is tummy time. Exactly how it sounds, this is supervised time laying on their tummies. This enriching activity supports core muscle development as children develop the strength they need in their back and neck for crawling, walking and eventually to be able to sit comfortably in a chair. From this position they will also experience a different world view, developing mentally and physically as they look around. Being increasingly in control of these movements is also deeply gratifying, enjoyable and confidence boosting. Before we had knowledge of sudden infant death syndrome (SIDS), parents would often put babies to sleep on their tummies. Now the advice is to always put a child to sleep on their back, so babies no longer spend hours in this position. However, supervised tummy time, from as early as two months of age, is an important and enriching activity for you to offer (Figure 2.2).

Figure 2.2: Exploring the world one tiny adventure at a time! Tummy time is strengthening all the core systems, as well as offering a unique look at the world.

Once they have grasped crawling by about six months old, next comes pulling themselves up on objects, and cruising as they develop the muscle and bone structure, as well as the mental acumen to begin walking. You won't need to do much to encourage this in children but do be mindful of effectively discouraging it through constraining their movements, for example by strapping them in a chair, or by offering sedentary alternatives, such as sitting in front of a screen.

Play

During the early months your babies' brains are growing and developing at a rapid rate – a rate that will continue to increase until they are around three years old, when it will be more densely packed with connections than at any other time in their life. We will look at this in more detail in the next chapter, but for now know that children are making these connections and learning about their world through the experiences they are being permitted. And much like all other mammals, they are doing this through play. For example, they are learning about the laws of physics when they play with cause and effect. You will recognise their enjoyment of this realization every time your older babies throw their hat, toys, dinner, or anything else close to hand. The enjoyment of playing with what they can do and the effects of it are too rich to resist. From a very young age, babies will take joy in associating simple actions with a given outcome. Learning to behave in certain ways to get an expected result is known as operant conditioning and, at a basic level, is something children can do from the time they are born.

Even much younger babies have shown an understanding of how their actions impact the environment around them. In a wonderful experiment, three-month-old babies were shown to realise that it was their actions that controlled the movement of a mobile suspended above them. Laid in adjoining cribs, a ribbon was secured to each of the ankles of two infants, however only one ribbon was secured to the mobile at its other end. For a few minutes both babies kicked and watched the reaction, but soon the child in control kicked far more often. And was seen to significantly favor the leg that was connected, becoming fascinated by the influence they had on the reaction. Even when they were brought back days later and neither child was in control of the mobile, they appeared to remember as they responded in just the same way.

Understanding

Understand the impact adults have on this process through every interaction

From the time they are born children are seeing, hearing, thinking creatures, reaching out for your social interactions and using every means they have available to draw you in. It is then so important that you engage with them, as you connect on every level. While they may not seem to be understanding very much and certainly will not be responding with conversation in the traditional sense, they are taking in everything you have to say. In fact, their only limitation in their ability to communicate with you is through the immature coordination of their vocal tract; this has nothing to do with their ability to take it all in.

Communication

The more speech a child hears, the better they become at this fundamental process. But as I have mentioned, this must be a two-way exchange as children engage with others and have them engage back, developing the necessary techniques needed to communicate. To make sense of language and converse with others is then a far longer and more involved process. Whilst this won't begin in earnest for a few months, the skills they need for it are being rehearsed through every exchange and do then depend on the amount of interactive conversation a child is exposed to from an early age.

Conversation is then essentially an exchange, learning that there are times when you can speak and times when you need to listen. Researchers at Harvard University termed this a "serve and return" as they noted conversations moving between the participants. Much like a ball in a game of tennis, we serve a sound and wait for it to be returned before serving again. But speech is a tricky thing to master. Long before babies have any words, they are trialing this backward and forward exchange for themselves. And as they develop this ability, babies need lots of opportunities to experience, hear and trial it for themselves.

Through these "conversations", you are also demonstrating the "exchange" of language. Remember, you can support a child with this process by changing your pitch and tone as you start and finish your sentences. As a child develops their ability to engage in the backwards and forwards "serve and return" rhythm of conversation, you can make it a game. Taking turns as you offer them cues that they respond to with babble before you talk back. You can even include physical action opportunities from the first months of a baby's life as you have fun with this engaging experience.

Research has suggested that children growing up within communication-rich environments hear in the range of 30 million more words by the time they start school than those children where communication has not been valued or offered. This is not achieved through technology, this needs to be human interactions, so consider where your children are getting these opportunities throughout the day. Do you value every change and feed? Do you automatically turn off excessive noise so that children can tune in to conversations? Do you talk to them when walking and exploring the environment? Do they have opportunities to interact with older children? These are all golden opportunities for conversation, even long before a child has words of their own.

Movement

Offering children a diverse range of physical activities allows them to benefit from the diverse benefits that they offer, even when you may be completely unaware of the good that they are actually doing. If you have pre-crawlers, you can see some of this fundamental work happening for yourself. Sit the child on your lap and have someone come from, say, the right-hand side to show them an interesting toy and they will look to the right to see it. Do this a few times so that they get used to seeing the toy come from over their right shoulder.

Then turn your chair 180° to face the opposite direction, and approach with the toy from the same side, which is now on your child's left. One of two things will happen. If the child has not yet learnt to crawl, they will tend to continue looking over their right shoulder for it. A crawler, however, will correctly now look to their left. So, what is going on here?

Once a child has developed their ability to move around their environment, they are no longer the centre of everything. Instead, they are moving around within a three-dimensional space. Before, their brains were coding egocentrically; everything was according to their body position and they expected the toy to remain over their right shoulder. Once they are mobile, however, the crawling child can now demonstrate a world-centric view. This requires them to map their world differently, adapting their worldview once their newfound mobility brings with it all kinds of new opportunities. This shift in the way their brains are coding information is used in experimental studies to demonstrate the work children do through their experiences of movement.

Crawling and reaching, for example, especially when this crosses the midline of the body, have been strongly associated with the emergence of certain mental abilities. Studies using technology to offer young infants the physical support and mobility of a much older child have seen their mental reasoning accelerate in line with the physical skills that these supports have enabled. However, today's lifestyles can see children restrained for too much of the time, delaying children's development as is seen by the later onset of crawling. While different cultures follow different practices that you may need to be aware of, once a child has independent mobility, let them use it. Whether this is through crawling or bum-shuffling, once they can engage in free exploration, self-control and coordination, those synapses in the brain really start firing on all cylinders. When thought of in these ways, why would you ever leave a child strapped into a chair or in front of a screen for prolonged periods? These early years are a finite period and much of it is spent sleeping, so for the rest... get active!!

Play

All through childhood, children are wiring up their neural connections, their brain changing through the experiences it is offered. You can see this happening in your baby between the ages of about four and eight months. When you place a long, thin object, such as a wooden spoon or finger into your young child's hand, they will naturally grasp it with an overhand grip. But if you offer an object vertically, they will likely try to use the same grip which, this time, will not work very well. If you play this game between the ages of five and seven months, you will see an important motor milestone developing as they begin to orient their hand to match the position of the object before they reach out for it. After a couple more weeks, they will be able to adjust the positioning of their hand in a fluid motion as they reach for the object itself, mentally adjusting the size of their grip to match the intended object.

But to allow all this essential work to happen, children need to be stimulated with interesting and novel experiences. And they also need time to observe others, to reflect on their experiences as they assimilate and make sense of what they have learnt. They do then need a balanced environment with adults who understand their needs and can pick up on their cues. Research repeatedly shows that babies are quick to respond to novelty, so be aware of when they are interested and when that interest is beginning to wane, changing your approach or allowing them to rest. With practice you will become better at picking up on these cues that they will be quick to communicate to you. As they get more verbal, engage in "conversations" as you play, allowing your reactions to be influenced by their responses as you let them practice the "dance" of spoken communication. Children are very good at letting us know how they feel, whether it is a baby turning their head away, a toddler physically and verbally demonstrating their growing feelings or a teenager being quick to leave the room. But we do need to be in tune with them.

Support

Be supported to reflect on how you engage and play with a baby, developing the opportunities they need for deep-rooted physical and cognitive development

By the time a child starts school, the early experiences and introductions to communication that they have had in these first months of life will make a significant difference to their first days in the school classroom. Impacting their social skills, their vocabulary and their ability to communicate, these experiences have a huge bearing on how well the child will settle, establishing new friendships as they interact and bond with their peers and the new adults around them; giving them the skills they need to not only understand the lesson but to get involved in it; and contributing ideas and asking for the help they need. Their abilities to communicate, engage and play also go on to affect the friendships they are able to make and keep, along with having a significant impact on their happiness, sense of security and well-being.

Supporting babies' communication

Firstly talk to children, a lot. From day one. Surrounding children with language makes a huge difference to the numbers of words they hear – and as a direct result, the number of words they can recognise and in time, use for themselves. But more than this, it surrounds them with the rhythms and patterns of speech and language, allowing them to become familiar with these long before they have words of their own. Communication, however, is more than knowing words and how to use them. To support a child's communication, they also need to be actively heard. So, listen as they discover their thoughts and feelings and show them that they are worthy of being heard – even when all they are communicating with is babble (Figure 2.3).

Figure 2.3: A child is surrounded by a sea of sights, sounds and sensory stimulation. So be mindful of this throughout your environments.

You may like to introduce some baby sign language. This set of simple hand gestures or signs takes the complexities of speech away, leaving a child's mental resources available to concentrate on the message they are trying to communicate. This gives children a way of being understood that is deeply gratifying and further enhances the bonds between you. There was some original concern that teaching children baby sign would in some way hinder their speech development. However, these fears have been unfounded as children's spontaneous speech and use of language has shown no delay. In fact, babies have been shown to speak earlier and in longer, more complex sentences when they have known baby sign first, and this is quickly left behind when its use is no longer needed. Even a few words will offer them a different way to communicate from a very young age, with benefits being seen in many areas of brain development.

Ideally, avoid screens during these early years. Sensory stimulation is hugely important to a developing child, but this needs to be a two-way exchange. Screens will never be able to adequately offer this, but they do manage to detract children's attention away from it very effectively.

Supporting babies' movement

The UK government suggests that babies under one year old should be encouraged to be active throughout the day, every day in a variety of ways. They suggest that if a child is not yet crawling, you should encourage physical activity by offering incentives to reach and grasp for, to pull and push. You can do this by propping them up comfortably and safely, then offering an array of interesting objects. They do not need to be expensive toys; many household items will do the job just as well.

- Encourage their body movements as you speak to them from different positions

- Display things of interest around the environment and allow things to move naturally such as reflective items hung where they can move in the wind

- Promote their body movements as you encourage stretching during your daily routines and full body movement during supervised floor play

- Encourage mobility through a variety of safe and supervised play environments as you explore all kinds of conditions and sensations

- Offer them tummy time from the first months of life as they develop their vital core systems in ways that are essential for moving and controlling their body as they get older

- Allow them to sit comfortably, to navigate the environment and to join in with activities requiring stability and balance

- As they begin to find their feet, make a "cruising course" to motivate independent explorations

Most importantly, avoid keeping babies secured in a chair for any longer than absolutely necessary. At this very young age, children need to be given the opportunities they require to feel what their growing bodies can do (Figure 2.4). Every moment they are strapped in, they are prevented from strengthening their muscles and bones. With a limited number of waking moments during this first year of growth and development, do all you can to avoid squandering them.

Figure 2.4: Every time they explore their environment bones, muscles and sensory systems are developing in ways that make the experience too enjoyable to resist.

Supporting babies play

From an early age, if you want to stimulate a child's mental development through the play you offer, you need to consider the opportunities they are given and the senses that these experiences are engaging. However, do be mindful of what can become completely overwhelming as you consider the environment you are in. Overstimulation is too much for children to manage, meaning the opportunities for further sensory stimulation you are offering may cause them to become upset or shut down with no developmental benefits. You might then like to consider some of these questions as you reflect on the environments you are offering.

- What different kinds of noises are they hearing, the more subtle and distanced as well as those directed towards them?

- Are they encouraged to change their focus from objects close by to further away?

- Are they touching different textures, consistencies, and temperatures or are they all plastic?

- Can they smell dinner cooking, a lavender scent bag, or a familiar perfume?

- Do you offer them different flavors to try? Even freshly cut lemons offer rich sensory stimulation.

There are many wonderful resources, toys and games on the market. But as they change with every season, we can lose sight of certain staples that should feature heavily in every child's toy box. There is a reason that so many of us have fond memories of playing in the kitchen with pots, pans and wooden spoons or a little older and finding ourselves absorbed in a grandfather's tool shed with some old bits of wood and tools. It is no wonder that so many commercially bought items are all reinventions along the same theme.

The idea of offering very young children a range of "bits and pieces" to explore and investigate, to combine and manipulate, is nothing new. Treasure baskets now offer this idea within many childcare settings and, whilst potentially staggeringly expensive, this is the best resource you can offer to a young child. But it need not cost you anything. Essentially, no different to what has been offered to babies for generations, this is a basket full of colours, textures and materials, devoid of plastic or manufactured toys and offers babies endless combinations to explore. As they gain mobility, these can become themed and include containers as they play with cause and effect, problem solving and repetition. So collectively, have a rummage around the home and that of friends and family as you acquire a rich array of objects.

As you play, connect on every level as you surround babies with the cognitively and socially enriched environments they need to develop the communication techniques, physical skills and mental abilities that they will later depend on. Make sure they have lots of linguistic input, plenty of chances to talk back in real and meaningful exchanges. Offer them the encouragement they need to move, stretch and bend their bodies, to consider the world around them and the impact they are having on it. And keep it fun!

I am also often asked about babies' exposure to screen time. The American Academy of Pediatrics (AAP) continually recommends that all forms of television and entertainment media should be avoided for infants and children under the age of two and then no more than two hours of total screen time per day. When you consider how many hours infants spend sleeping, feeding, changing and engaging in everyday routines, this does not leave much time for all the essential experiences their developing brain needs. While a screen may effectively hold a young child's attention, it offers no real mental, physical or social development and crowds out the positive developmental activities and social interaction with other humans that they do need. So please, enjoy these amazing years of development, engagement and connection with your children and leave the screens alone.

3 Striking the right balance

Caring for children is a complex business, with so much to think about and be concerned over – some of which is meaningless worry that does little more than keep social media pages busy and you up at night! But in some respects, there is much you can do that will make a huge difference to a developing child through the choices you make, the interactions you enjoy and the practices you introduce as you care for children and prepare them for life.

Children need a safe environment in which to grow physically, emotionally and socially as they gain a sense of who they are. They need opportunities to explore their own choices and to learn from their own decisions and their mistakes, within an environment of calm understanding. They may behave different to how you may have expected, or how their friend behaves, but these too need accepting and respecting as you get to know the whole child (Figure 3.1). As they grow and develop in mind and body, children need the experiences that will support connec-

Figure 3.1: When we get down to a child's level, sharing in a moment, we are developing deep attachments of trust and meaningful connection.

tions to be made, to strengthen muscles and bones and to inform them of how and why change is occurring. We have learnt that sensory experiences and diverse, rich stimulation is important, but that too much can be a negative experience, causing children to react negatively, shutting down and retreating from any potential benefits. So, what is important? Where is this growth occurring and what can we do to support it without overwhelming it?

As a child grows and matures, their rate of development in some areas may differ from others. Taking longer to master something that others find easy, perhaps learning to walk before some but struggling to speak when others begin chattering away. Along the way

DOI: 10.4324/9781003327073-4

they will be looking to the key adults in their life for guidance and support. But an overbearing "helicopter" style of caring for a child, quick to jump in as soon as a struggle is detected, will take away a child's ability to cope with change when someone is not there to take control. This denies them the experience of seeing what they can do for themselves or what it means to persevere when things are not easily achieved.

From the moment a child is born they are equipped with some primitive structures already established in their brain. To complete the structures they need, they are looking to the influential people, experiences and environments around them for guidance. While this may sound a little haphazard – after all who is to say that these people, experiences and environments will be positive ones? – it is this amazing ability to adapt to the environment we are born into that has allowed humans to become the only species that can live and flourish within every environment on the planet. So, how does brain development happen and what is actually going on?

Knowledge

Know how the brain is connecting in the early years and the importance of every experience to a growing and developing baby

When we smile into the face of a young baby, it is all too easy to become captivated by the newness of this preverbal, pre-mobile dependent. But we would be wrong to overlook the immense rate of rapid development that is going on during every moment of these extremely sensitive first years or underestimate the impact all of this is having on their future growth. Dependent on every experience they are given, it is vital that we are aware of how we can enhance their opportunities and how we can read the signs that things are becoming too much.

Growing a child's brain

It is amazing to think as you look into a baby's eyes, that even when newborn, they already have most of the 100 billion neurons or brain cells that you have contained within your adult brain. And yet, at birth, their brain will have been around a quarter of the size of yours. So, what is changing? Where is this growth and development coming from and, as influential adults in their lives, what difference are we making within this process? (Figure 3.2).

Figure 3.2: When we have strong attachments, a child can feel safe and protected in our care. This allows the brain to concentrate on everything else that may be going on.

The growth that is occurring comes from the microscopic connections being made between the neurons. It takes somewhere in the region of 1,000 trillion connections to wire up an adult brain. And these connections are being made through every single experience a growing child is exposed to – whatever that may be. Once made, these connections or synapses control how the neurons interact with each other, which in turn informs a child how to think, how to move and how to behave.

Every time we offer a child an experience or give them something to look at, we are encouraging these synapses to fire. Every feeling we stimulate within them through their environment, through the care they receive or the responses of others around them, is causing these connections to be made. Every time you engage you are responding to their early attempts at engaging with you. They are developing mental pathways that will inform them of how they should respond next time. During these moments you are laying the foundations for social expectations and informing their responses, directing how they should react to external influences, now and into the future.

Surrounded by empathy and love, a child is equipped to empathise with others and to form meaningful connections. When they experience appropriately managed levels of everyday stress, they learn to regulate their emotions and cope with the ups and downs that every day brings. And when they see their instinctive attempts at learning and exploring met with support and encouragement, this fosters a love of learning that will see their mental and physical health flourish.

From the very beginning, every experience impacts a child's learning potential. As one experience informs how they respond to the next, foundations are being set for the rest of their life, impacting their future learning and development, as well as their health and well-being, their likely success at school, even their future life trajectories more profoundly than where they live, the resources they have available or the income of the home. And when these experiences are lacking, their future opportunities for learning and development are deeply affected. So, rather than reaching for the toy catalogue or website, understand the difference you can make when you offer enriched, powerful experiences from the very beginning.

Eager to learn and keen to understand

Every child is living in a three-dimensional world of people, plants, animals and a whole host of things to engage with and make sense of. Whatever their location, whatever their situation, whatever the year, a child is surrounded by voices to interpret, social skills to understand, dangers to be aware of and emotions to fathom. This is an awful lot of things to learn within bodies that are growing and developing daily, changing how they feel, how they respond and how they can move. Because of this, they are born with a brain that is eager to learn and hungry to make sense of their world. This powerful motivation to learn will see them driven to explore and understand their surroundings, even when you wish they would not. While they will be touching and mouthing everything within their reach now, in a few years they will have found other ways of exploring their environment and the relationships within it.

To understand all of this information, children are born with some primitive structures already established in their brain. You will have seen this when a baby instinctively knows to grasp your finger, to turn their head as their cheek is rubbed, or the way they will fling out their arms and legs when they are startled. These are known as primitive reflexes and are hardwired into every new life as a survival mechanism. Other kinds of knowledge, a baby must learn along the way, such as what happens to their toy when they can no longer see it or why their friend seems to be experiencing an emotion that they themselves are not feeling. While their friend seems upset, they themselves are quite happy now that they have the red trike!

Whether you consider pulling over a pot of paint a desirable experience or not, the learning opportunities for a child are just too rich to resist. It is only when their efforts are fruitless or met with resistance that they learn not to bother. When they are denied the experiences that they are naturally motivated to pursue, a child will experience frustration. They will then try alternative methods, but if this continues then annoyance and eventually boredom will follow. And with these emotions comes some more difficult behaviours as the child learns what it means when they try to pursue their need to know and understand. So, if you want to protect a child's motivations for learning – and your paint supply – provide children with experiences they can explore and investigate from day one, creating the deep connections within their brain and achieving the growth they need in the areas that are being stimulated.

The importance of connections

So, how important are the experiences we offer to a growing and developing baby? How can this have any impact on their developing brain and does this in any way explain why children behave in the ways that they do? Like I said, with every experience you offer to your youngest children, you are literally growing and developing their brain through the connections being made.

With such vital processes occurring it is understandable that children are compelled to obtain every experience possible. If you were to place a cream cake within grabbing distance, it is unlikely that a baby will consider the reach to be too much bother. And when they have a fist full of sweet smelling, sugary delights, they instinctively know the next set of receptors that they can make best use of. And while you may think, "Fair play, I would probably do the same thing", take a moment to remember that their immature brains are not quite as discerning as yours. You will probably see the same response with anything unlucky enough to be within grabbing distance.

This also explains why a child's mind needs to be stimulated. If not by you, then through any means necessary. If they are prevented from doing so for too long, for example by being left in a sedentary position, they will soon become fractious. If their attempts at engaging with others are denied, for example, if you appear disinterested despite their every attempt to engage, they will quickly become upset. But too much of a good thing can become exhausting. Luckily babies are very good at letting us know when they have had too much. We just need to make sure we are ready to listen.

Understanding

Understand basic brain development and how this is impacted through every choice you make

When we stop for a moment and consider how much a child needs to learn from their first moments of life, we can begin to see the monumental task ahead of them. And the importance of any influence that we may have on this process. As children begin to understand this boggling world of depth and texture, sounds and emotions, relationships and expectations, we need to consider how and where all this growth and development is taking place. And how we can support them as they make the connections they will rely on.

A world of opportunities waiting to be explored

Our mature brains have learnt to translate a multitude of sensory information coming at once from our eyes, our eardrums and our fingertips. Once our brain receives this sensory input, it systematically rearranges and transforms it, using memories from our past experiences to create a complex yet coherent interpretation that allows us to operate in this complex world. We can make out the face of a loved one in a crowd, we can make sense of a conversation in a noisy environment and we can make decisions and act on them.

We have become so good at all these complex processes that are occurring continuously and simultaneously that we take them for granted. Until something goes wrong, that is. But just like many other skills we have learnt along the way, this takes lots of opportunities to practice. As a baby strives to take in and process all they need to, their young brain is around twice as active as yours and at times this can be overwhelming. This reaches a peak at around the age of three when they are more connected and more flexible than at any other time of their life. From this point on, the brain becomes selective in the connections it keeps. Those connections that have been triggered more often through the experiences they have had are considered to be more important while others are reduced through a process called pruning, a stripping away of seemingly unnecessary connections, allowing the brain circuits to become more efficient.

While some of the basic wiring has been predetermined, for all the rest, children rely on the experiences they are provided with while looking to those who are more experienced around them to know what they need, guiding them towards the experiences that matter and the opportunities they need to explore them. The experiences a baby is exposed to in these early months is then instrumental within this process. The choices you are making, the experiences babies are having and the emotions they are feeling are forming these connections, through the good experiences and the bad. Every one of them is changing not only the hardwiring of their brain, but also the ways in which they will react to new experiences and new opportunities (Figure 3.3).

Figure 3.3: Whilst children need a sensory stimulating environment, they also need moments of calm and relaxation as the brain processes all it has experienced.

Making sense of it all

During these first years of life, much of a child's fundamental brain growth will have occurred, with more than one million new neural connections being formed every second as the brain undergoes a rapid period of development. Triggered through every experience, like with us all these are received by the child through their senses. Through their touch, sight, and hearing and through their sense of taste and smell, this sensory input is then processed in the cerebral cortex, at the front of the brain, along with their thoughts and feelings. This explains why a learning experience is enhanced when multiple senses are combined and why our senses can be so powerful at triggering an emotion – I cannot smell coconut without thinking of holidays on the beach or hear music from the 1980s without being whisked back to my childhood. And when multiple senses are involved in an experience, even more connections are being made.

The experiences a child is exposed to then makes a massive difference within this process and the choices you make are essential. From the times you sit together and connect as you play instead of turning to a screen; when you walk to the playground talking about the sounds and smells all around you, rather than travelling without communicating; even that time you took your shoes and socks off just to feel the wet grass between your toes. Through these experiences you are changing not only the hardwiring of their brain, but also the ways in which they will react to any new experience and the new opportunities that come their way.

They are learning to deal with every new situation, informed and enhanced by every previous experience they have had of something similar. They are learning what to expect from the people they meet and the reactions they might expect from their own actions. And they are also learning about where their efforts and attention are best placed. During these early years you are literally growing and shaping a child's brain, defining them as a person in ways that will be with them for life. So, embrace every opportunity as you play, engage and experience this amazing world of sights, sounds, smells, tastes and textures together.

Developing unique brains through unique experiences

At a fundamental level, children are essentially experiential learners. This means that their knowledge and understanding of the world comes from every experience they have within it – the good ones and the bad. Their developing knowledge and understanding of how the world works, the skills and abilities they are gaining as well as their expectations of what they can do and how others might respond to their actions; but more than this, as these connections are made, they are then informing the child's expectations of the next one (Figure 3.4). Like I said, while some of the basic wiring and structures of their brain will have been predetermined at birth, something like a 1,000 trillion connections are now needed as they begin the processes of developing their own, unique adult brain through every single experience a growing child is exposed to, whatever they may be.

Figure 3.4: The world is full of sensory stimulation and experiences, every one forging deep connections within the brain.

As babies strive to make all these connections, remember that this is a learning process, one that they will be seeking out many repeated opportunities to try. While you may know what will happen when you bang your hand down on the spilt milk, they will be making, testing and reinforcing these ideas of cause and effect. Connecting sight and sound, understanding how their arm feels as they move it through the air, the sensations felt in their hand and the forces required for a good slapping sound. They are also exploring the responses they are receiving from those around them. Especially when this triggers an emotional one, so if a child close by laughs at what they are doing, they could be there all day!

Support

Be supported to implement the key practices that will make all the difference

As you consider the phrase "Preparing a child for life," many different things may come to mind. You may think about personal qualities and life skills that you would wish to bestow upon a child, reminiscent of good fairies over the crib of Sleeping Beauty. You may consider professional skills such as the ability to be financially independent, to set and achieve their goals whilst remaining motivated and engaged with all the world has to offer. You may think about their ability to lead a happy and healthy life as you consider the "gifts" that appear top of your wish list, maintaining a positive attitude and bouncing back when life throws adversity their way. You may consider the strength of their relationships to be significant, alongside their ability to engage well in social situations while taking care of themselves as they actively make healthy choices.

In some instances, the differences we make to our children take root very early on. What may seem only a slight or barely considered change in our behaviours can have a staggering impact when you view them over the long term. If you consider, for example, the child who is not experiencing a conversation-rich environment during their first months of life, how are they going to be ready to speak themselves, to know how to engage in a conversation or to take an active role in it? If a child is not experiencing the things they can do, feeling the ways they can move or seeing the effect of their ideas, how will they know what they are capable of? It is then so important that we offer children the wide range of diverse experiences they need to explore. And as we have seen, these are received by the child, through their senses.

Nurturing babies within sensory rich environments

As we have seen, sensory learning, especially multisensory learning, is hugely powerful. This explains why young children make such good use of it and why we should seek to do likewise. Studies have shown that children raised in a sensory-rich environment, where they have been given opportunities to engage in positive, sensory rich experiences, develop brains more densely packed with the connections they need for healthy brain growth and development. So, with the neuroscience to support it, how do we go about offering this hugely influential process of learning to our children?

Firstly, the important thing to remember here is that early childhood is a critical time for brain development to occur. As I have mentioned, at around three years of age, as processes of synaptic pruning identify the experiences that are worth keeping hold of and those that are not, any core experiences that have been missed during this vital time will not easily be replaced. You will have experienced this if you have ever tried to learn a new language as an adult, something young children seem to pick up with ease. Or, if you have spoken to a child from a language-poor environment who is now struggling to acquire the speech patterns they are going to need for school. So, think for a moment of the experiences you are offering to a baby and the senses that they are using when they engage with them. Consider the resources you offer them to play with, the materials they can touch and the environments they find themselves in and the opportunities they offer to see, hear and smell.

- Do you have plastic toys, or a range of metal, wood and fabrics with different textures, temperatures and responses?

- Consider whether their touch, sight or hearing, or their sense of taste or smell are being engaged… or could they be?

- Do you offer them real fruits and vegetables to explore? Perhaps slicing open a juicy orange as they experience the vibrant colours, the smell, the juice trickling through their fingers as they grasp its slippery texture before tasting. Or do you give them a pretend one?

- Do you make use of the natural world and the sensory stimulation it offers? Do you go outside so they can feel the wind in their hair?

- Think about the sensations they experience throughout their bodies. Are their feet encased inside a sock and shoe or can they feel damp grass or warm sand between their toes?

- Do they have lots of opportunities to engage in positive experiences where they can try different things and be rewarded for their efforts?

- Is their environment rich in language? This does not mean teaching them five languages before they are five but talking to them. Having conversations and really engaging, using a wide range of words from the time they are born.

- Do you speak with children throughout the day, during every routine as well as by sharing books and stories, nursery rhymes and songs?

- Are there lots of opportunities for social interactions, with different people of different ages in different situations?

If you can provide these opportunities, their developing brains will be sure to encourage the rest. And remember, when multiple senses are involved, more connections are made, so allow children to combine different senses, along with processing their thoughts and feelings. But also, be aware of over stimulation by being in tune with their need for space and opportunity to blow off steam, to relax and just be.

How much of a "sensory rich" environment is too much?

By definition, childhood and especially early childhood, when much of the foundational and structural brain growth is occurring, only lasts a very short period of time. To take advantage of this, children are born ready to learn and eager to acquire the many skills they will need over the coming years. We have learnt how the brain's growth is strongly affected through a child's experiences of their world and the people in it and how critically important your nurturing care is within this process as they depend on you to offer them the opportunities to develop these skills, especially before they gain the mobility and access to their environment for themselves.

As we strive to give children all they need to become independent and ready to lead healthy and successful lives, it may be tempting to fill every moment of every day with deeply enriching opportunities. But there is a limit, however, and children of any age are very good at letting us know when they have had enough. When an experience becomes overwhelming, it will begin to trigger a negative response that, if you miss the early signs, you cannot fail to notice. In the very early days, a young baby will react quickly to too much stimulation, letting you know in no uncertain terms that something needs to change.

In these moments, the thinking region of the brain begins to shut down, leaving the child functioning from the more emotionally reactive lower brain where their primitive functions reside. As their immature brains are only just beginning to develop beyond these functions, they are quick to revert back to them, being quick to cry when something becomes too much to handle. As they get older, other techniques can be learnt and utilised before needing to deploy these primitive defences. Eventually the adult brain can, hopefully, have a range of responses to try when a situation becomes too much, before we kick and scream because someone took our favourite toy. These emotions and the behaviours they trigger are deeply impactful within a child's learning journey and we will look at these again in future chapters.

Stressful moments will be a part of every baby's life; as they wait to see if someone will remember to feed them, as they wake alone in a room wondering if they have been abandoned, or when they feel they need changing, wondering if they will ever be warm and dry again. And like I said, for a baby who knows they are essentially powerless at the best of times, this can be terrifying. When they experience this stress, cortisol is released into the body preparing it to act. And provided this is short lived, it will cause little affect as it disperses into the blood stream. The trouble comes, however, when a child frequently finds themselves in a stressful environment. For healthy growth and development to occur, a child cannot devote excessive energy to managing their levels of stress and ridding the body of these hormones. They need a calm, safe environment with plenty of opportunities to play and explore. They need adults around them who are aware of how their bodies and brains are growing, who speak to them, play with them and care for their needs before the child needs to worry. They need to be valued and nurtured in an environment adapted to suit their needs, responded to sensitively and protected from sensory overload.

Exposure to excessive stress can have long-term negative consequences for a child's developing brain, affecting the development of their language and communication, their emotional stability and their chances of succeeding in school, work and relationships. If you have concerns that a child is receiving less than the optimal balance of stimulation, be mindful of these outward signs. Monitor their developmental milestones and be ready to support them with the care and intervention they may need.

4 Time for Rest

Whether you have ever been the parent of a newborn or worked to support young parents, you will be familiar with how exhausting this time of early life can be. In the first weeks of life babies do not have much of a sleep cycle. Certainly not one that is linked to day or night, or the established sleep patterns of most families. And despite the stories you may be told of the child who slept through the night from day one, it is far more typical for babies to wake every few hours, regardless of how tired their families are feeling or the plans they may be derailing.

Accustomed as we are to a full 6–8 hours, when our sleep becomes repeatedly disrupted for any reason, it can be a challenge. While one night of interrupted sleep is unlikely to have much effect, over an extended period of many weeks this can have a heavy impact, disturbing the rest of the whole family. While you are not about to change the biological demands of a newborn any time soon, it is important to balance the needs of everyone in the home. But what can you do to ease the situation when a child continues to cry through the night?

Some advice will have you believe that a crying child is simply demanding attention and any response to their demands will only add to this. Others will suggest that not responding to their cries for help will reinforce feelings of abandonment, with lasting damage. In truth, both are a little bit true and with informed guidance and support you can help establish a middle ground that is right for everyone.

Knowledge

Know what is happening to our bodies and minds when we sleep and how much sleep children need at different times in their lives

Getting enough sleep is vital to all our complex internal systems. So important, in fact, that even after just a few nights of insufficient sleep we will feel the detrimental effects

DOI: 10.4324/9781003327073-5

on our bodies, our minds and our general sense of well-being. Without a constant level of upkeep, these fundamental processes are denied and the body soon feels the problems associated with insufficient downtime. We feel less ready to take in our surroundings, to concentrate on new information or to process the messages being received from all around us. It affects our positive moods and the energy levels needed to benefit them as well as our ability to respond to the experiences of a new day, let alone to engage with them.

The body's need for regular sleep

When we sleep, the body undergoes a series of changes that are vital to our overall health. When the sleep-wake cycle is not well managed or it has been thrown off by irregular sleep routines or inconsistent bedtimes, the effects are felt throughout the day. You may have experienced how this feels after a prolonged period of broken sleep or the jet lag experienced after foreign travel. For a child without a well-managed sleep cycle or routine, these feelings can become prolonged. Over time this can then result in long-term detrimental impacts to their general health, well-being and engagement in all things.

As a child closes their eyes and drifts off to sleep, they no longer need to operate at such a high level of awareness. This allows their brain and body to slow down and engage in processes of recovery and assimilation (Figure 4.1). When they sleep, memories from the day are consolidated and transformed into more durable formats, ready to be moved into the child's long-term memory storage. Repair and maintenance systems also kick into high gear as the important upkeep of their bodies and mind takes

Figure 4.1: Regular periods of deep sleep are just as important to the developing brain as every experience you offer to a child.

place, promoting renewed physical and mental performance, ready for when they wake. With lasting effects into the short, medium and long term, this goes some way to explaining why sleep deprivation feels so bad to all involved.

We all have an element of natural routine in our lives. Physical, mental and behavioural practices that follow a daily cycle set by our internal body clock are known as circadian rhythms, and they allow essential functions and processes to quietly carry out in the background. One of the most important and well-known circadian rhythms is the sleep-wake cycle. While we might assume this runs on a 24-hour clock, research involving the natural sleeping and waking patterns of people temporarily removed from all knowledge of the time saw this settle into more of a 25-hour rotation. We do then need to reset this internal clock every day, which is why successful sleep at night will benefit from a good supply of natural sunlight first thing in the morning.

Knowing our sleep cycle

When we sleep, our brains move between the four stages of the sleep cycle. Stages one, two and three are in non–REM sleep, whereas stage four is in REM, named for the presence of rapid eye movement that is occurring. In stages one and two of non–REM sleep, our eye movements will slow down, as will our heart and breathing rates, and our body temperature decreases. These stages are a very light form of sleep from which we can be woken easily. Once we enter stage three, our sleep becomes much heavier. This is the most refreshing stage of sleep and is when the body releases the hormones needed for growth and development. If we are woken in this phase of the cycle we will feel groggy and disorientated, knowing we had been in a deeper form of sleep.

In stage four, the final REM stage, our eyes take on the rapid movements the stage has been named for. Our breathing and heart rate becomes faster; this is when we will have our most vivid dreams. And it is this stage that is most important for our learning and memory function. By the time a child is around four years old, one complete sleep cycle will last about 90 minutes. This is similar to our own cycle and is why we are advised to sleep for a multiple of this time; five cycles (seven and a half hours) together with half an hour to settle into sleep for the typical eight hours a night, or perhaps eight cycles (nine and a half hours) for a child.

A baby's sleep cycle is much shorter than ours, with longer time spent in REM sleep. With their sleep patterns more intricately linked to the needs of their bodies than ours might be, this tends to be the system that is calling the shots. And as they need to eat every two to three hours, regardless of the time of day or night, this tends to be what governs their sleep. Because of these more frequent periods of "little and often" sleep, infants do not always reach the deeper levels of sleep that we enjoy from our prolonged cycles of rest, meaning that they may also be easily woken. As frustrating as these cycles can be, this pattern of sleep is of great importance to their developing brain and will continue to varying degrees until they are about three years of age when their brain reaches around 90% of its adult capacity. As they grow, a flexible sleep schedule combining nap times and bedtime routine can be established that can adjust to the needs of the growing child and their family. But for now, when a sleep-deprived family becomes aware of what is occurring it can go some way to easing the pain of managing it.

How much sleep do we need and when should we be getting it?

Evolutionarily speaking, we evolved to sleep when the sun went down, becoming as quiet as possible as we retreated from others and the potential dangers around us until the sun came up once again. Now that we have electric light and little fear of predators, this need to withdraw is no longer there and we can stay awake for longer. However, this does not take away from the body's need for long periods of uninterrupted rest. Anything with a complex nervous system needs to sleep, this includes all mammals, even fish and ants.

When a child is first born, their newborn brain is immature and cannot wait long before performing the maintenance processes that take place during sleep (Figure 4.2). Along with a regular need to be supplied with food in the early months, their sleep schedule will be set to accommodate these tasks, regardless of the more established sleep patterns of older members of the household. As they get older, they will settle into more established cycles of sleep but for now, regular short periods of rest are to be expected.

Every child is different, but experts do offer a suggested number of hours of sleep to guide a growing family, combining night-time rest and naps. But these figures tend to be derived from studies that show the amount of sleep children get, rather than what they need which is more difficult to quantify. So, be wary of advice that seems to suggest otherwise; these estimates vary considerably and can be misdescribed.

During their first month it may seem like a newborn baby is sleeping continuously or at least

Figure 4.2: With substantial growth taking place, essential processes for brain development need to occur regularly, meaning other systems need to temporarily pause. What we see is another nap time!

throughout the day; however, this should settle to around 14–17 hours during the first three months. By the time they reach their first birthday, their need for sleep will have decreased to between 12–16 hours, before dropping to 11–14 hours during this following year. Between the ages of three and five, this tends to decrease again to between 10–13 hours and then to between 9–12 hours during the pre-teen years.

While our teenagers may seem to want very different sleep schedules, they do still need their full 8–10 hours. As their brains mature during puberty they can stay awake for longer, which may seem to fuel a desire to stay up late, a decision that is regretted when they need to sleep later into the morning. But don't simply blame late-night viewing habits; the melatonin that affects their circadian rhythms is now being secreted later at night than it was when they were in earlier childhood. And rather than fighting this familiar teenage angst, we and school timetables would be better placed simply understanding it.

By 18 months old a child may start resisting daytime naps, but the important thing here is to know the individual child in front of you. If you are struggling to settle a young child down for their afternoon nap when they want to be doing anything but, ask yourself who this nap is for. Do they need it or do you? That is not to say that scheduled rest times during a busy day of hustle and bustle is ever a bad thing as we all strive to manage the needs of the body without resorting to excessive amounts of caffeine, sugar or chocolate.

Understanding

Understand sleep cycles and the importance of establishing routine

While a small baby's sleep and, more importantly, waking cycle may bear little resemblance to the sleep that the rest of the family may want to enjoy, eight hours of unbroken sleep each night is an unrealistic goal during the early months. And striving for it may do little more than add to a family's growing frustrations. A baby has a small tummy and they will get hungry. They have tiny bladders, meaning they will get wet. And at these times, no method you introduce is likely to be of much help.

That said, a family that allows a child to simply fall asleep whenever and wherever they decide in the absence of any constructive routine is going to be introducing problems that will take a toll on everyone. And while the need for a routine is so important, if this has been going on for a while, you may now find yourself trying to support an overtired child, struggling to understand why things have changed and in the absence of any concept of a routine. So, with realistic expectations for now and optimistic plans for the future, look to establish a flexible sleep schedule from day one, combining nap times and a bedtime routine that can adjust to the needs of the growing child and family. This begins by understanding the importance of doing so.

The importance of establishing a sleep routine

As we have seen, our sleep patterns are directly influenced by the environmental cues around us. The circadian rhythm that lets us know it is time for rest responds primarily to the light and darkness in the environment and helps determine the pattern of our sleep-wake cycles. It does this by influencing the production of melatonin, the hormone that makes you sleepy. As our natural circadian rhythm is more like 25 hours than the 24-hour day we live by, we need to reset this clock every day when we see the sun, making it especially dependent on the daylight we are exposed to first thing in the morning. Production of melatonin is also triggered by the amino acid tryptophan, contained in the breast milk a mother produces in the evening. So breastfeeding where possible will result in sleepier babies after the evening feed, helping to establish a breast-fed baby's circadian cycles.

Properly aligned, our circadian rhythm promotes consistent and restorative sleep, as well as affecting eating habits and digestion, body temperature and other important bodily functions. But if disrupted, for example by the bright lights of a screen at bedtime, it can create significant problems affecting physical and mental health. Listening to soothing music or reading a book is far more effective at easing you into a good night sleep. The best way to establish a child's circadian rhythm is then to provide lots of sensory and behavioural cues in phase with the 24-hour cycle we live by – in other words, by establishing consistent routines, especially in the lead up to sleep. While a very small baby will have little consideration for the routines you have in mind, they will start establishing behavioural patterns by the time they are around four or five months old. And once in place, you can then begin to establish and maintain some consistent sleep time routines by the time they are around six months old.

When a child has become used to the patterns of behaviour introduced during these first years of life, they can gradually learn to take on more of the routine for themselves. As they establish their own mental and physical habits around sleep, healthy decisions about bedtime can develop and increasingly be turned over to them. And as they become more responsible, a healthy regard for their sleep needs can be established.

But as important as routine is, so too is life. Everyone has times when they struggle to fall asleep, nights when something is weighing on our mind, or we

Figure 4.3: Establishing familiar routines on the lead up to sleep helps the body begin the processes of relaxing down and getting ready for rest.

just need that additional hug. When you have structure in place, you can afford to have flexibility (Figure 4.3). Do not worry about sticking to routines on rare occasions when an exciting opportunity arises; grasp it and enjoy the memories you are making because of its irregularity. Just be sure to retain your regular habits during the rest of the time.

The effects of not getting enough sleep

If you are, or have ever been, struggling with irregular sleep patterns yourself, you will know that the effects of irregular sleep routines or inconsistent bedtimes are felt throughout the day, impacting children's success in school and the achievements they are likely to realise. So, establish healthy mental and physical habits around sleep times that start with playing outside in the morning. Advanced technologies that are used within sleep studies consistently link sufficient sleep with a range of short- and long-term benefits that we need to be mindful of – especially as we support children to establish the patterns and behaviours of healthy sleep.

When a child develops a healthy sleep cycle and is no longer waking frequently, they can enter the deeper levels of sleep only accessed once the body has established its 90-minute cycles. A few hours after they have fallen asleep, once in deep sleep important hormones for growth and development are released, as well as hormones controlling appetite and blood sugar levels. The physical growth of the body is then regulated during these deepest stages of a child's sleep, illustrating the need for uninterrupted periods of deep rest.

With too little sleep, ghrelin, the hormone for feeling hungry, goes up and leptin, the hormone for feeling full, goes down. This explains why, if you are sleep deprived, not only do you tend to reach for the calories you hope will provide the energy boosts you need, but your hormones are also out of balance. When a child has this hormonal tendency to overeat through lack of sleep, they may establish patterns and tendencies that are inclined to remain with them for years to come, with lifelong impacts on their health and general fitness.

Like I said, every child will be slightly different in their need for sleep, but a child who isn't getting enough may well offer you some familiar signals. When they are very young, they may appear hyperactive during the day and yet, rather than being full of enviable levels of energy, appear cranky, whiny, irritable or moody. They may seem to zone out or fall asleep during the day. They may struggle to pay attention or have difficulty following simple tasks, all of which may lead to difficult behaviours. So from day one, begin establishing healthy sleep patterns in your children.

Trouble finding sleep

Even with the best laid plans and intended routines you may hit stumbling blocks. This can often happen at around nine months old when children will typically go through a phase of interrupted sleep. But know that with the right processes in place, this too will pass, ready for the next curve ball they will undoubtedly throw your way. However, if you are struggling to establish a routine with a six-month-old, there may be some additional issues to consider such as the physical conditions they are being settled in or an underlying health issue such as acid reflux.

You may also have unrealistic expectations about the amount of sleep a child should be getting or when they should be getting it. To know how much sleep a child needs you need to pay attention to that child. You can loosely follow the guidelines, but it is more important to be flexible and look for the signs the child is giving you. Keep a diary of when they have slept and the behaviours and temperaments that follow. Also consider the exercise they are getting, the routines that are being followed and the time they go down for a nap. A late night does not reliably result in a late morning!

Support

Be supported in ways of encouraging children's sleep and how to ease them back into it – now and in the years to come

Bedtime routines can be as individual as the family in which a child is being raised. However, studies regularly show the benefits of consistency and some sort of structure that a child can settle themselves into. And at all ages, this starts with good routines that are regular, with plenty of warning and that follow an expected plan. Whether this is for yourself, your own child or you are supporting a family with a child who is struggling, begin by being mindful of the full number of hours of sleep they need for their age, then draw up a plan and begin getting ready for it with enough time to complete the stages with a minimal level of stress.

Establishing a sleep routine

Routines need to start some hours before you expect a child to settle down to sleep as you provide sensory and behavioural cues in phase with the 24-hour cycle. Begin by establishing consistent meal times, during which you can set and clear the table in the same way. As you introduce familiar routines you are establishing patterns within their mind of what is to come. And as they get old enough, involve them in these routines as they are more fully experienced.

Play familiar, gentle music before sleep instead of busy or flashy images on a screen. Singing too can soothe babies and signal an end to the day. During this time of slowing down it can be tempting to turn on a screen as you relax together or get on with other jobs. However, the blue light emitted from screens is one of the worst things you can give a child in the hour before rest. Instead, establish a routine that may include clearing the table and washing up as you play familiar, gentle music. In the evenings this can be followed with consistent bath time routines, getting into pyjamas and brushing teeth before cuddling up together on the bed to read a book. All of which is adding to the rhythms and "bedtime rituals" you are establishing as you create a pleasurable shared experience that you can both look forward to.

Be quick to go in or leave to self-soothe?

Some suggest that children simply need to learn to self-soothe and should not get used to your continued company on demand, while others may advise that you are reinforcing feelings of abandonment by not responding to their cries for help. In truth, both are a little bit true and you need to establish a middle ground that is right for the child and the family.

Being too quick to rush in will deny a child the chance to develop the skills needed to settle themselves back to sleep. If a child keeps waking, this could be the result of a sudden jerking awake if they are very young. Jerking in our sleep is something we all experience. But whilst we will typically fall straight back to sleep, a baby with their lack of motor control will be more likely to tense up, flailing their arms and legs and disturbing their sleep. If they wake prematurely, wait a moment to see if they soothe themselves back to sleep. If not, you may need to reassure them with your presence that all is well and they are not alone. Do not put on the light or engage in conversation, simply settle them down and leave.

Sometimes children will wake briefly for no apparent reason. They may cry to alert you of their presence although there is nothing wrong, realise this for themselves and fall back to sleep. At this point, provided they have developed the skills to do so, they will settle themselves and fall back to sleep. However, if you have been too quick in the past to rush in, they may need some support in getting back to this point.

You can allow a child to cry for a few minutes to see if they will self-soothe, but before they become too upset, go to them. Do not put on the light or engage in conversation, simply reassure them with your presence that all is well and they are not alone, settle them down, perhaps with a soothing pat on the back and leave. If the crying continues, you can soothe them in the same way again, without picking them up. This may go on a few times but if you are firm and consistent a baby will learn to go back to sleep without you, realising that crying is not getting results. You can then progressively leave longer periods of absence before they need reassurance and they will eventually learn to ease themselves back to sleep. While this process can be emotionally challenging, both for you and the child, it is a short-term path to much less disruption in the long term.

If you have considered and resolved all these possibilities it could be that your crying baby is simply feeling separation anxiety, a normal stage of development happening during this time. Being too quick to rush in will deny a child the chance to develop the skills needed to settle themselves back to sleep. Cuddling, feeding or talking when a baby wakes during the night may simply encourage them to wake regularly for this attention. However, if their cries are uncharacteristic or have been going on for up to 15 minutes, always investigate. A baby left to simply cry themselves to sleep will do so eventually, but this is more about exhaustion and learning the futility of seeking reassurance rather than any healthy habits of self-soothing or long-term benefits of sleep training.

And then, just when a little one manages to sleep through the night, they become a slightly bigger one and can start experiencing the joys of sleepless nights once again. While everyone has times when they struggle to fall asleep, nights when something is weighing on our mind or we just need a little reassurance, be careful of difficult habits forming. Active sleep management can help families reset these processes or put some new ones in place that will see everyone gets the sleep they need in the long run.

Getting older and still struggling

Toddlers are more aware of their surroundings, so distractions in the environment might be disrupting their sleep time. Their growing imaginations may also be starting to interrupt sleep. So, now more than ever, setting simple and consistent routines is the best way for getting a sleepy toddler snugly into bed. And as they become more aware of the tricks they can use, remind yourself of how important it is to set the rules and stick to them as you consider how many times you'll get the toy they throw from the crib in defiance of bedtime. This not only helps achieve better sleep now, but also helps when more serious problems arise in the future.

If an older child is struggling, look again at the environment you are expecting them to sleep in and the distractions it might contain, including its light, noise and temperature levels. They may be pushing their covers off during their sleep, so consider the temperature of the room or what they are dressed in. Is there too much noise coming from another room? Toddlers will learn to sleep with some noise, but loud play and activity or too much conversation close by can be disrupting. Consider the exercise they have had during the day, especially outside with lots of fresh air and sunlight (Figure 4.4). Could they be hungry, in need of changing or feeling unwell or overtired? And be patient: if you have been without a sleep routine for some time, it is going to take a little while to establish this. But the impact on everyone's health and well-being is definitely worth the effort.

Figure 4.4: Physical exercise, especially first thing in the morning sun, is the best way to begin establishing healthy sleep patterns.

As they get older, it might be bad dreams that are causing disrupted sleep, especially for a toddler who has a hard time telling these from reality. It is unwise to tell them that their dreams are not real; their dreams are very real – they have just experienced them. Instead, be open and respectful of their emotional experience, give them a hug and let them know they are safe. Acknowledge that dreams can be scary, that you have scary dreams too sometimes. But that you also have fantastical dreams, where you can go places and do things you can never do when you are awake and that you know you will always wake up. Be mindful of the books you share just before sleep, keeping the content mild and perhaps introduce a comfort item to help provide reassurance.

You can also help an older child to know their own body's need for sleep as you ask yourself whether your expectations of them sleeping at this time are realistic. Start by offering a nightlight so that after the established routines they can continue to read until they feel ready to fall asleep. This may initially result in some late nights, but they will soon learn to respect their body's need for sleep that will stay with them into the teen years and beyond. And you can always offer some intervention if they begin to appear overly tired. And please, encourage all screens to be removed from children's bedrooms!

5 Understanding babies' responses

The ways in which a child reacts to any given situation is dependent on many different things. It will depend on the gene pool they have been born into and the environment they are in. It will depend on their developmental stage and developing character, whether they are naturally anxious, prone to anger or susceptible to hurt feelings. It will be affected by current family stressors and life circumstances, such as moving home, family break ups, new jobs or the birth of a sibling. And it can also simply hinge on the fact that they are feeling unwell, tired, frustrated or merely hungry.

Simply said, emotions are a natural, healthy and necessary part of growing up that we want our children to experience – at the right time and to the right extent. Trouble comes, however, when their emotions are not well managed or when unrealistic expectations are in place. Children have so much to learn and comprehend and their emotions need careful understanding, guidance and support from the adults around them. Throughout the *Nurturing Children* series, I will talk about children's developmental milestones and the structures that need to be in place. These include the importance of routines, interacting with others and learning to share. And we will look at how, once these are all in place, children are better equipped to manage their responses, to choose their behaviours and to negotiate the inevitable conflicts that are a natural part of growing up. All of this begins by understanding children's emotions and the responses they trigger.

Knowledge

Know how we experience our emotions and the ways this affects children and their sense of security

It used to be thought that during pregnancy an unborn child was somewhat of a passive bystander, protected from negative influences of any physical and emotional environment by the placenta. However, studies show that this is not, in fact, the case, with

DOI: 10.4324/9781003327073-6

effects from the mother's diet, emotions and levels of stress all influencing the development of an unborn child in ways that can have long-lasting effects. For example, research by the Developmental Origins of Health and Disease (DOHaD) show that when a mother does not receive enough nutrition during pregnancy, the baby's systems can adjust for a world that is lacking in nourishment. If they are then born into a world of plenty where more than enough nourishment is consumed, significant issues may arise. This effect is being considered as a reason for the rapid increase in obesity and type 2 diabetes in some nations.

Other studies have recorded post-traumatic stress symptoms in large numbers of pregnant women following extreme, prolonged weather conditions, acts of war and periods of famine, after which higher numbers of babies have been born with a small head circumference at birth, a good indicator of brain volume. Children born of mothers pregnant during such times have been studied for decades, with participants more prone to anxiety and depression from an early age and into their teens. Lower birth weights, decreased fine motor skills and lower intellectual abilities have also all been noted in these children.

How and when emotions develop within a child

From birth a child is experiencing and expressing their emotions. They will show anger and outrage at being allowed to feel hunger. And then, moments later, express joy and happiness as they nuzzle into the warm arms of someone offering them a feed, gazing adoringly into their smiling face (Figure 5.1). Evolutionarily speaking, the development and demonstration of a child's emotions has clearly been an important part of their earliest moments, securing the relationships they have needed for their own survival. However, despite being remarkably good at feeling their emotions, at this very young age a child is less equipped to manage them. This work does not really begin until the toddler years when they start to develop a stable sense of themselves as separate

Figure 5.1: At this age, emotions can feel all-encompassing. It is then so important that we offer a calming presence as everything in the world stabilises again.

from the other people around them. As this happens and a child seeks to find their own place in the world, this comes with some strong ideas about what it is that they want, which you might be familiar with.

As a child gets older, they move from relying on their significant adults around them to balance their emotional state and look more to their peers as they begin to learn how to manage their emotions and solve their own problems. This new sense of self also means that they are beginning to feel some new, self-conscious emotions such as pride and embarrassment for the first time. When these toddler years arrive, you will see some of the most pronounced periods of development and growth. And with them, some rapidly fluctuating emotions, in much the same way as you might expect from the teenage years when the emotional outbursts of our overwhelmed toddlers are often revisited.

By the time a child is four or five years old, their emotions are noticeably more developed. They can now experience mixed emotions, such as being angry and sad at the same time and will begin to use their emotions as an unconscious defence mechanism. Along with this maturity comes the ability to have simple conversations about their feelings. And with support, you can guide them as they begin to learn alternative coping methods when a situation causes their emotions to rise.

By the time they are ready for school, a child will be able to think about and discuss their emotions in increasingly sophisticated ways. This allows them to use cognitive coping strategies, such as distraction or self-talk as they find methods that will help them to think through their emotions and calm themselves as things become more difficult. But this also means they are becoming better at hiding their feelings. Whilst this can be a good thing within a social interaction, it also means that you may need to look more closely at their behaviour to see the emotions that they are masking.

Feeling our emotions in the ways that we do

The emotions a child is feeling will have a great impact on the way they perceive their environment and interpret the events of the day. But then, is that not the same for all of us? Researchers at the University of Pennsylvania interested in this question took a group of people experiencing various emotions, asking them to rate these beforehand. They then showed this group of people two different pictures in rapid succession. One depicted a funeral scene, while the other showed a lavish feast. Those within the group who had previously been classified as currently experiencing depression remembered the funeral scene over the feast in significantly higher numbers. This suggested, they concluded, that when we are feeling low, we tend to focus on the negative things around us. The trouble is that these reinforced feelings of negativity can then see us spiral into deeper negative emotions.

Starting the day feeling anxious can soon feel like everything from the spilt coffee to the burnt toast is going against you, with knock-on effects until bedtime. If you are in a critical mood it can seem like everyone is criticising you, and what may have seemed like a witty reply yesterday can be heard as a cutting putdown today.

Not only do our emotions deeply affect our outlook, but they also translate to those around us. Especially towards our children who are looking to us to offer a sense of emotional direction and a calming rudder to their less mature, often fraught emotions.

If you are feeling frustrated when a child needs you, you may model being short tempered and dismissive, informing not only the child's behaviours and emotions, but also their developing methods of managing them. If instead we can focus on the positives around us, embracing a happy emotional disposition, feelings of happiness may well be constructively reinforced. Whilst feelings of negativity and certainly clinical levels of depression are far more complex than "deciding to see the bright side", for the little things, this is worth actively considering. As you also remember, the children around you are responding to all the emotions they feel and see.

The effects of our emotions on our children

Emotional development is a complex process that begins in infancy, continuing and refining well into adulthood. Within this process, children need to learn what feelings and emotions are. They need to understand how and why they happen and to know that they are neither good nor bad, they just are. We all have emotions and we should not be afraid to feel them. However, children will need help to recognise their own feelings and those of others, developing techniques and effective ways of managing them when they see them arise. All these processes are important for their emotional well-being as they develop the skills they will need to manage their emotions for life.

In the early days, the emotions babies experience are pretty straight forward as they experience joy, anger, sadness and fear. These are simply felt to prompt the necessary responses to secure their safety, to obtain the things they need and guarantee their survival. But as natural as they may be, this doesn't stop them from being terrifying as the child spirals around these central motivators (Figure 5.2). A little older and, as they begin to develop a sense of self, more complex emotions like shyness, surprise, elation, embarrassment, shame, guilt, pride and empathy are felt. Still very young, these emotions will be felt primarily through physical symptoms such as their racing heart or butterflies in

A Young Child's Cycle of Emotions

Fear
What if I always feel this way? There is nothing I can do... no one is coming!!

Joy
No worries, all is good with the world again!

Anger
How dare I be allowed to feel this way... something must be done!!

Sadness
I did have joy, but something doesn't feel quite right...

Figure 5.2: A Young Child's Cycle of Emotions - For a very young child this constant search for safety and survival can be a terrifying process that repeats every time they feel hunger, tiredness or in need of a change.

their tummies. These responses are triggered by the hormones that are now flooding their young system and will require energy and emotional resources to be dispersed. When a child is growing up in a very emotionally charged environment, or where their needs are not being well looked after, their body spends a lot of time and energy ridding itself of these hormones, to the detriment of other things it could be doing.

By this point children are also becoming more aware of the people and emotions around them as their own emotions become influenced by them. As they will be spending most of their time with their family and perhaps other key adults and children within a childcare setting, this is where these influences will come from. Through these relationships children will notice certain responses associated with emotions. Are they seeing repeated behaviours when someone gets upset? Do they receive a hug or frustration? Are they connecting certain emotions with a need to act in a given way, maybe to run away or hit out? Are certain values and beliefs about appropriate and inappropriate ways of expressing their emotions being conveyed? As they mature, children will develop their ability to recognise their own feelings, but this starts by noticing the feelings being demonstrated by others. If negative associations are being noticed around them, what does this tell them about their own feelings the next time they have them?

Understanding

Understand the processes going on inside children when they experience strong emotions and what happens when these are not effectively managed

How do we feel our emotions?

When we have a particularly emotional event, thought chemicals are released into the body to inform us of our response to it. As we experience the world or even think about it, the neurons in our brain release these chemicals to trigger reactions in the body that we feel as emotions. They can be anything from a slight flutter felt in the tummy to a debilitating physical reaction. Happy and empowering thoughts produce chemicals to make us feel happy and empowered whilst negative, sad or angry thoughts produce chemicals that make us feel sad, angry or depressed. When in a healthy balance, these processes inform our responses and empower our reactions, getting us out of the way of danger or letting us know where we need to be. Trouble soon comes, however, when these emotions are unmatched to our need for them.

Take fear for example – that all-too-familiar feeling of a racing heart and rapid breathing as hormones flood the body, triggering these responses to ensure higher levels of oxygen. Preparing the fight-or-flight response to the danger it perceives, this system is effectively readying the body for action. It's a healthy reaction when that perception of fear is accurate, but feeling heightened levels of fear or anxiety long before an active response is needed is not a healthy state to be in. Think back to the last time you had to wait weeks for a test result. Feeling anxious about a transition or big changes at home can fill a child's body with these response hormones long before they are required for any positive effect.

Affecting children even before they are born

When we experience stress, cortisol, the stress hormone, is released into the bloodstream as the body readies its reaction to the perceived threat. This starts very early. Like other substances, cortisol can cross the placenta from mum to the unborn child. If this is a rare occurrence this will have few ill effects; however, if an unborn child is repeatedly exposed to high levels of stress, their cortisol responses will adapt, preparing for a world that their mother has perceived to be stressful and potentially hostile.

This adaptation will affect the way a child manages stress and experiences anxiety. This limits their ability to concentrate and maintain attention, affecting behaviours in similar ways to the signs of conduct disorder (CD) and attention deficit hyperactivity disorder (ADHD). Like I said, this adaptation to threat could be lifesaving when a child is born into a hostile world where their levels of focus and excess energy, heightened fear and readiness to react with alert aggression is needed for their survival. However, if instead they are born into a more typical life, where they are required to concentrate and pay attention with more stable emotions, they are going to struggle. These children are often found to react with heightened emotions, they tend to be quick to cry, to appear helpless or to react with anger. Now imagine this child sat in a school classroom.

The importance of breaking unhealthy response cycles

A predisposition to negative thoughts does not develop because of one negative emotional incident. However, over time, processes in the body establish a chemical continuity and this emotional predisposition is created, intensifying over the days, weeks, months or even years that it is left to reinforce. These patterns begin laying down from a child's earliest experiences, ready to inform all their future responses.

If the adults and family members surrounding a child are predisposed to anger, they are likely to react to most situations with an automatically angry response. Their own experiences of being parented will be informing how they themselves are parenting. Informing their child's experiences, which are now in turn, forming the memories that they themselves will later reflect on. They are even being coded into the genes that are being passed to future generations.

Unless these patterns of behaviour are consciously changed and different behaviours actively chosen, these traits will continue to be passed on. To override this genetic expression takes a great deal of active mindfulness and a huge effort of will. However, the importance of breaking these unhealthy response cycles is too important to not offer the support and guidance that is needed – ideally before a child is even conceived.

The self-perpetuating thinking and feeling cycle

We all have negative thoughts from time to time. Often these will be fleeting, other times they may last for some time. When a negative thought continues for hours or even days we might call it a "bad mood" with no permanent damage. However, if a bad mood continues, perhaps for weeks or even months it can become a more deeply ingrained temperament that is much harder to find your way out of. When a child is consistently experiencing the world and their responses to it in a particularly emotional way, predispositions to those emotions can then develop. Understanding how behavioural and emotional health problems arise in our children allows us to better address the issue at a time when we can actively help them to manage it.

Every time a child experiences strong feelings, chemicals are introduced into their systems. If they are repeatedly feeling frustrated and angry, they become more conditioned to that emotion as chemical receptors within the body adapt, potentially establishing patterns of responses that are harmful for their body and overall quality of life.

In a child, you might see the beginnings of an ingrained temperament as a tendency to whine, to be quick to cry or quickly resorting to aggressive responses. If this continues unchecked, with the child continuing to experience the same negative thoughts and emotional reactions, a self-perpetuating thinking and feeling cycle can establish as an emotional predisposition or a personality trait develops, fuelled through the continual emotions that are felt and the behaviours that are prompted and being learnt from (Figure 5.3).

A SELF-PERPETUATING

Thinking and Feeling Cycle

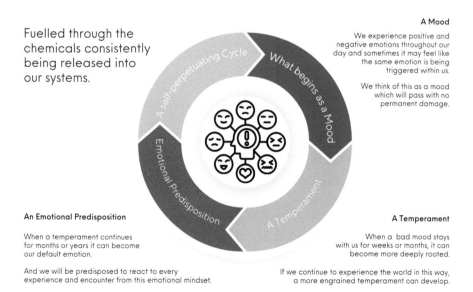

Fuelled through the chemicals consistently being released into our systems.

A Mood

We experience positive and negative emotions throughout our day and sometimes it may feel like the same emotion is being triggered within us.

We think of this as a mood which will pass with no permanent damage.

An Emotional Predisposition

When a temperament continues for months or years it can become our default emotion.

And we will be predisposed to react to every experience and encounter from this emotional mindset.

A Temperament

When a bad mood stays with us for weeks or months, it can become more deeply rooted.

If we continue to experience the world in this way, a more engrained temperament can develop.

Figure 5.3: The Thinking and Feeling Cycle - Every time a child experiences strong emotions, chemical receptors respond to manage these within the body. If negative emotions are continuously felt, the body adapts, ready to respond to the expectation of more negativity.

With less and less conscious control over their emotional reactions, this simply becomes a part of who they are. These emotions can then trigger behaviours that may be confused by a diagnosis of ADHD and the like, with medications all too quickly prescribed. Symptoms can range from feeling fearful or self-conscious, to experiencing nervous anxiety or feeling worthless and unloved unless they can attain a level of perfection. Without intervention these feelings are likely to escalate, leading to mental health issues that may stay with them for a lifetime.

With diagnoses of anxiety, depression, conduct disorder, attention deficit disorders and hyperactivity becoming increasingly common, our children are struggling. With suicide rates on the rise in many countries we must then look to support the mental health of our children without simply seeking to medicate behavioural and emotional problems away. And with a child's expectations and understanding of the world informed through every experience of it, you need to be mindful of them from day one.

Support

Be supported as you develop the early stages of emotional intelligence and take active steps to break negative emotional cycles

As we have learnt, children are feeling and expressing their emotions from the day they are born. As they get older and develop a greater sense of themselves as part of a bigger, more complex world, these emotions and the behaviours they trigger become more involved. Especially when children start coming in closer contact with others. Children will be deeply passionate about things and emotional outbursts can become an all-too-familiar response. If a favoured toy breaks, a four- or five-year-old may be distraught with grief. If another child broke the toy, even by accident, the original owner might be furious and an emotional outburst may well be the hasty and regular response. It takes time, support and guidance before they can learn how to regulate these strong emotions that are all a part of growing up.

Establishing emotional intelligence

From an early age, it is important that we help children to develop their emotional intelligence. Far from shielding them from negative experiences, this involves allowing them to experience their emotions, even the negative ones. In time, as they learn to identify, understand and manage their emotions and the behaviours they prompt, a stable sense of mental security can establish as negative emotional predispositions can be avoided.

However, their depth of skill in handling these situations will depend on their ability to monitor both their own and other people's emotions, to understand and label the different emotions being shown and to use emotional information to guide their thinking and behaviours towards them. Before a child can understand and respond adaptively to another person's emotional experience, they need to be able to manage their own. And this takes strategies of emotion regulation, allowing a child to regain control over their emotional state as they rethink a situation and focus their attention on reasons to feel happy or calm, such as a time when their immediate feelings of anger will have passed.

Reframing negative thinking and feeling cycles

In the moments after any strong emotional reaction, we have a small window of opportunity in which to decide how we are going to react. This is known as the refractory period and it allows us to make a choice about what happens next. Within this period, you can actively support a child to alter their perspective and return to a state of calm through conscious thought. In the first years you are not going to be discussing a child's conscious thoughts with them. But you will be establishing their memories and frame of reference for when this becomes a conscious thought process. At this stage, this is all about modelling positive behaviours and surrounding babies with calm emotions and considered responses.

If children are seeing negative thinking repeatedly cycle into negative feelings that are then negatively expressed, these destructive cycles will begin to impact how they themselves think about and perceive their own emotions, affecting the actions they then take and the person they are becoming. While you may think you are effectively hiding this from young children, believe me, you are not. Children are very good at sensing the emotions of others from a very young age. As their greatest influence, you need to be aware of the messages you are inadvertently sending.

Breaking the cycle

When you feel yourself becoming excessively emotional about a difficult situation, you need to reframe the moment. Look for the positives, try to put things into perspective or decide to pick the battles that are worth becoming upset about before the situation becomes too much. If you have already passed this window of opportunity, look to step out for a moment while you take a breath and consciously encourage positive chemicals to be released into your bloodstream as you look to evoke more positive emotions.

While this may seem easier said than done, ask yourself "what is the alternative?" Difficult moments happen within everyone's life and you have the mental capacity to see the bigger picture or imagine a time when this moment will have passed in ways that the small child in front of you does not. If we do not take these active steps to calm our negative thoughts, they will continue to release negative chemicals that will in turn initiate further negative emotions. And without this active form of intervention, negative thinking-feeling cycles will continue automatically.

That is not to say we want to shield our children from negative emotions. They are just as necessary and valid as the positive ones. The right level of fear when approaching something dangerous is an automatic response that may well save their life. However, too much fear and a predisposition towards anxiety may start to develop. Equally happiness, joy and love are emotions every parent would want for their child, but experienced unquestioned and unchecked within some relationships could see them staying in a situation that they would be better off getting out of. And there are times when we all feel angry; trying to eliminate anger is neither possible nor desirable. It can be destructive, but it can also motivate us to change our circumstances for the better.

Teaching young children positive responses

Negative emotions are then a very real part of life. Looking to shield children from these is neither supportive nor developmentally helpful. Children will experience their own negative emotions and they need to feel able to do so rather than wondering what makes them wrong or different for feeling this way. They also need to learn ways of interacting with their peers when they are experiencing these emotions (Figure 5.4).

Figure 5.4: When we calm a child, we can help ease negative emotions out of their body before this becomes the way they expect to feel.

While you would never look to express anger in front of a child, it is ok to tell a child that the milk you have just knocked all over the table has made you feel upset. Show them that you do not want to feel this way, so you are taking active steps to feel better about these feelings, getting a cloth and cleaning the spillage up. And the help you received in doing it has made you feel really happy. All of this involves a large set of complex reasoning tasks from your adult brain. Unrealistic expectations of something similar from very young children is simply setting everyone up for some frustrating times that will do more harm than good. But you can model your responses to them, showing them the calming techniques you have learnt to support your own measured responses that they will in time, take their lead from.

Our job is to teach our children how to handle their emotions in healthy ways.

- Avoid shying away from dealing with difficult, emotional situations, no matter how tempting it may be

- Consider the lessons you are demonstrating for even the youngest eyes and ears around you

■ Model ways of taking a breath and calming yourself down from feeling angry, showing how this is an emotion we all feel from time to time, but that there are responsible and constructive ways of managing it

■ Model kindness and respect as you help children learn to communicate, even during fraught moments

When things become too much

The first thing to remember within any stressful situation or when the demands that are placed on a child become overwhelming, is that children are children. They have immature social skills, unmanaged physical responses, a developing unfinished brain and confusion about their needs and wants. Their brain is continually flooding their body with chemicals, causing them to act in ways that we may often read as quite irrational and chaotic. And as well as all of this, every child is their own person, full of emotions and motivations and liable to getting things wrong. They are not programmable machines, even when you did "Exactly what the book said!" And I am sorry to have to tell you, but they will test your boundaries.

These early months especially can become a time filled with enormous demands and concern with information coming at you from every angle, much of which has enormous potential for misinterpretation. Try to keep a balanced perspective on things and take steps to manage, rather than add to, your stress. Where you can, take the opportunity to re-examine and simplify the demands you place on your own expectations. And prioritise and concentrate only on what is really important as you allow yourself the time to slow down and enjoy a child's early days. This time is too important not to.

The growing abilities you are establishing in children now as they learn to feel, recognise and understand their emotions will be instrumental in developing their future behaviours. And without these abilities and the practice they need to perfect, you will be hard pushed to begin considering the behaviours we will look at nurturing in the next chapter.

6 Nurturing babies' developing behaviours

As we learnt in the last chapter, from day one a child is feeling very powerful emotions that need recognising, understanding and actively managing. Depending on many factors, we saw how these are influenced by the way a child is feeling in the moment; are they hungry, tired or feeling unwell? Is the environment too noisy, overly stimulating or not stimulating enough? Pre-established influences on their emotional behaviours are also at play, a result both of their genes and all the previous experiences of feeling and observing emotions that they have been exposed to. These emotional dispositions illustrate the nature vs nurture argument you may be familiar with.

Every child, then, will respond differently when confronted with an emotional situation, whether it is their feelings of hurt or anger, excitement or joy that have just been aroused. Their reaction may also be different to the response of their friend, their sibling or even the way they would have reacted yesterday. As these emotions develop, they then have a more visible consequence. Seen within every behaviour the emotions trigger are the expectations they are forming of similar situations and the learned behaviours of the future.

As a child develops, they begin by obeying and responding to the influences of their own bodies. Heavily egocentric in these first months, they have little interest in what others are doing, having or saying; if they feel hungry they want to be fed now and they will use every behaviour available to them to make sure this happens as quickly as possible. A little older and their behaviours become influenced by what is going on immediately around them. They learn to behave as they are told to in the moment and, in time, learn to conform with others and follow rules as they fall into the socially accepted practices of behaving as others are. After this comes a more mature process as children behave in ways that they perceive as being right or wrong, behaving as they think they should (Figure 6.1).

DOI: 10.4324/9781003327073-7

Throughout all of these processes, children need structure and rules in order to feel safe and secure. This is not the same as looking to control children, a familiar technique used in many behaviour management strategies. So, take a close look at the underpinning processes involved with any behavioural guidance methods you may be considering. When you scratch the surface of many popular techniques you will see that these are based on methods of control. Instead, look to connect with children, allow

Figure 6.1: As a child becomes more aware of those around them they are watching and learning how to function in this social world.

their thoughts and actions to inspire you. And when their behaviours become difficult, look to understand why this might be and the support you can offer to guide them.

Knowledge

Know how behaviours develop and the effects we have on development when we respond to a baby in different ways

Before trying to understand the behaviour of a child, you need to know that most behaviours are, at least in part, instinctual. This may seem obvious when we think of a very young baby reaching out to be held or picked up, but actually, this remains true throughout our lives. Rather than being carefully thought through and considered in the moment, most of our human behaviours tend to be ingrained as a learnt response that we swing into before thinking too much about it, informed instead by all our past experiences. Each experience informs the next, a process begun in very early childhood.

When caring for a child it is then vital that you understand how their behaviours are developing and the importance of how you respond to them. A good example can be found when offering a healthy balanced diet and knowing the factors that may influence how receptive a child's behaviours may be towards all your efforts. How you then respond to these behaviours as you present them with a bowl of healthy pureed carrot is informing them about how they might respond the next time you approach them with the orange delight. And with these patterns of behaviour embedding at every mealtime, there is much you can do to establish healthy patterns of behaviour before you reach the highly opinionated toddler years and encourage their continuance in the years to come – provided that you do not fall into some common traps.

Developing healthy behaviours through the experiences of our ancestors

When we respond to anything, there are so many variables to consider that if we stopped to think about it all we would never do anything. Think about the last time you chose the behaviour of making a cup of tea. Did you consider the best way of heating the water to the temperature you would need? Would this be best achieved using a pan on the stove, a microwave, a hot tap or did you just flick the kettle on? Did you consider all the receptacles you could use, or did you grab a mug? Did you think about whether you might prefer milk, lemon, sugar, green tea or black, loose tea or a bag… or did you just make it the way you always do? And this is the tip of the iceberg. How about the time you have to drink it, the possibility of it being spilt, how others may feel about you having it, the number of tea bags left in the cupboard. The list is endless and these are just the external factors you might think about. Imagine the effects that drinking that tea had on your body?

To get by we do then rely on our past experiences and in some cases, the experiences of generations; for example, when it comes to the fundamental processes that govern the nutrition we take into our bodies. These deep-rooted behaviours are not only governed by all our own previous experiences, but also the experiences of millennia. As a species we have been around for about 200,000 years, evolving and adapting so that we may survive on this highly diverse and changeable planet. It is a process we became so good at that we are the only species to be able to inhabit every environment in all its extremes of temperature and available sustenance.

For most of this time we were hunter gatherers, following migrating animals and managing changing seasons as we experienced times of abundance and times of scarcity. However good times currently were, famine could always be close by. To manage this fluctuating availability of food we developed cravings for calorie-dense foods, storing up any abundance in fats and firmly establishing our preference for sweet flavours. The trouble comes today when periods of scarcity to balance overindulgence are a rarer experience and it is not often that you need to run across the savannah before enjoying your next meal.

As a hunter-gatherer, we would also have had to find out what is edible, mostly through experimentation. While we needed to take food into our bodies to survive, to eat the wrong thing could have killed us or at the very least, have resulted in a very miserable time. This is going to make you adapt your behaviour, becoming cautious about what you eat – especially if you are a child with less reserves. So children, or at least those who survived long enough to pass their genes onto children of their own, developed less adventurous behaviours around food. Some researchers believe that the age ancient cultures are thought to have stopped breastfeeding coincides with the age children were old enough to know to be cautious.

How do children's behaviours develop?

While our emotions and the way we feel about something may be instant, the way in which we behave is something we choose. No one can determine how you will respond to something; you are in control and you are responsible for the consequences of that choice. This is a lot for our children to learn. And with immature feelings driving these behaviours, this is an active choice that they will need to learn to take control of.

As our children experience what it means to make desirable and socially accepted choices with their behaviours, they need guidance, time and patience from us. As they learn the behaviours that are appropriate within a given situation, they need to understand what it means to take responsibility for the things they do. But for a child who is so often powerless within a situation, it can be difficult to choose how to respond when they do not feel in control (Figure 6.2). On top of this, they are not experienced in recognising or naming their feelings or the emotions surrounding them, nor do they have a long history of experiences and consequences to draw on.

Figure 6.2: When we repeat the ways we do something, such as reading a book together before sleep, a child's world can become a little more ordered as they learn the behaviours that are expected.

When we acknowledge a child's feelings as real and legitimate, without passing judgement, they are given the space and permission to experience them. Only then can they learn what to do with them. This is then a vital part of nurturing a child's sense of security in the early years, as we teach them how to recognise the feelings that are surging through their bodies. Once this is achieved, you can teach a child how to purposefully manage their behaviours and regulate how they respond to anger, fear or hurt feelings with the time, experience and practice they need.

Understanding

Understand a baby's need to feel secure and how this drives their behaviours

In the first months of life, a child's immature understanding of their emotions will not be driving their behaviours. Instead, they will be coming from a far more primitive place that relies on their instinct to protect themselves. We all need to feel secure, but whereas we can take any number of steps to achieve this for ourselves, a very young child relies on us to do this for them, and the only trick they have to motivate your actions are their behaviours.

Their behaviours are then rooted first and foremost in their need to feel safe and secure. Until this is well established, a child cannot turn their attention to anything else. Once a child feels secure they can then take the necessary risks to reach out to others and forge new relationships. They can explore their environment and try new things. And through their feelings of security, they can develop their sense of independence, of feeling powerful within their body and environment.

Developing feelings of security

The strongest sense of security for a very young child comes through the attachments that have formed with the significant adults in their life. In the early months and years of a child's life they begin to take notice of the people who are responding to their need for safety and security. Every time you give them a feed, make them feel warm and dry again, even when you gaze into their eyes and smile you are reassuring them that they are safe and loved and worth taking care of. From these acts the child develops a deep-rooted sense of attachment that they will, in time, use to shape the way they respond to the world.

These links to a caring adult are deeply significant in all moments, but especially when children begin to feel scared or angry, anxious or frustrated. These emotions can be all encompassing and they need an anchor and a guide to help soothe them and see them through this terrifying moment. Do not forget, children do not have a well-established sense of time; they struggle to imagine a time when they will not feel this bad. So, without you, it will seem that this is how they will always feel.

When it comes to the complex processes surrounding human relationships and the rules that govern them, these early relationships are a key part of their development. A child's opportunities for social and emotional connections must then be an important consideration during this time, both when looking to nurture their behaviours and as a foundational skill set that so much else will be built upon. Our behaviours showing them we are consistently available, offering physical soothing and comfort, helps a child to feel safe again. As a deeply influential role-model, we can share with children the techniques they need to return to a feeling of security for themselves.

Driving their behaviours as they respond with confidence… or run and hide

With this reliable sense of security growing within a child they can begin to turn their attention elsewhere, building a sense of confidence as they explore more widely. As their mobility increases this confident attachment allows them to roam further, knowing there is always a safe place to return to. They will look to test this frequently in the early stages, but less often with every time they easily find your comfort and reassurance.

These early experiences and the reassurances they receive develop a closeness between you. This may need testing again when they face a new fear or a bigger challenge, but every time you rectify a scary moment of separation or fulfil a need, their trust in you grows, establishing patterns of attachment that will inform all future relationships and offer a point of reference for developing successful, lasting relationships as an older child and on into their adult life.

While these attachments are a key influence on a child's sense of security, they are not a "fix-all". As was explored in the last chapter, how a child feels will fluctuate because of the time of day, the events surrounding them, or even a growth spurt or period of illness that you are not yet aware of. During these times even the most secure child might feel vulnerable and temporarily unsafe, causing their confidence to take a hit and their need for reassurance and added security to grow.

In these moments, a child's brain is detecting a threat to its safety or security. When this happens, it releases stress chemicals including cortisol to ready the body to react with "fight, flight or fright behaviours". Even though they may be surrounded by adults who are ready to support and nurture, the immature brain has evolved to respond to any perceived dangers with the instinct to protect. Their behaviour will display their feelings of anger, irritability, anxiety or withdrawal. They may also appear more emotionally immature when they are experiencing

Figure 6.3: When a child has developed a sense of security with you, they trust that new experiences will be enjoyable and safe and no longer a reason to be on their guard.

these stresses on their body. So, be more sensitive to the degree of nurturing they currently need, focus on the "secure base" that you offer to the child and do not be afraid to take a few steps back. Treat them as if they were younger if this is what they want as you nurture, without being overbearing or stifling. It will not last for long and they will soon be back to taking on new challenges from a place of safety and security once more (Figure 6.3).

Behaviours at lunch time

One of the first occasions a young child has for repeated opportunities to watch and participate in established behaviours is when it comes to food. Sharing a meal together is one of the oldest and most fundamentally unifying experiences we have, signifying peace, safety and harmony. For this reason, behaviours and rituals around food are a fundamental part of many celebrations and occasions. However, we can lose sight of these key opportunities to establish positive experiences of learnt behaviours if meal-times turn into a misdirected battlefield.

Today, children have a vast array of safe food options available to them to eat. But as I have mentioned, caution bred into us through evolution continues to see our little ones prefer to play it safe and mealtimes can all too quickly become a battle of wills. When it comes to young children, any negative experiences reinforced around food can remain with them for life. So, what should we do to prevent any unhealthy behaviours that might be established from becoming lifelong practices? And if a child is programmed through years of evolution to be reluctant to try new things, how can you raise them to not be finicky and to eat their greens? Well, the good news here is that as well as being predisposed to reach for food with a high calorie content, our bodies have also evolved to be drawn towards the things that it needs. Provided it has been introduced to them… and provided you know how to read the cues.

All babies are born with an established preference for the sweet taste of their mother's milk. You can try this by offering an infant a few drops of sugar water or a few drops of water flavoured with lemon and watch the reaction you get! But an even more refined sense of taste develops from the choices a mother makes during pregnancy. Pregnant mothers given garlic capsules or those who regularly ate carrots tend to have babies with a greater willingness towards eating these foods as they develop the tastes and preferences of their unborn child – another good reason to eat a healthy, well-balanced diet full of different flavours during these months.

In a study conducted in Philadelphia, 45 babies aged five-and-a-half months were fed green beans for eight consecutive days. Half the group were also given a helping of peaches, with researchers recording how much the children ate and the facial expressions that were pulled while they were eating. The peaches were, understandably, the preferred choice, with the children eating more of the sweeter option. As the green beans were eaten, a range of facial expressions were pulled that could easily be associated with distaste and for many parents result in foods being taken away. But the experiment continued.

As the children became used to the foods, the amount they consumed increased, with the green beans overtaking the peaches as their bodies learnt to eat more of what it needed. The continued exposure to nutritious food was increasing the children's desire for it, regardless of initial reactions. So, do not be put off by facial expressions, think more that they have simply not got used to it yet.

Support

Be supported in managing the triggers of behaviour, reflecting on the influences and environments you are offering

Supporting children as they learn to understand their behaviours and the emotions that trigger them is not always easy. And just when you think you understand these triggers, a bout of illness or the next growth spurt may change all of that. You may have carefully considered the environment and its influences, not realising that your expectations of them at this moment are more than they can manage. In their early years a child is not only trying to learn the behaviours that are expected of them, they are also learning how to manage their body, their feelings and their emotions. As they get a little older, they will also be looking to assert their individuality and their independence. Distancing themselves both physically and emotionally from those closest to them is a very natural part of growing up and understanding who they are in the world, but it does need careful understanding, informed guidance and support.

Helping children experience their behaviours without fear

As often as a child will fall as they learn to walk, they will make mistakes when learning how to behave. If you want to nurture a child's sense of security as they grow into a responsible, resourceful and resilient individual, you need to give them room to grow.

And yes, at times to make mistakes. Before their behaviour can mature, a child needs to have developed a sense of personal ownership, a sense of who they are and how they should act in the moment. But this inner sense of themselves cannot develop if all the control for their behaviours comes from the adults around them.

Children are also learning how to feel their emotions and how to make sense of the feelings that they evoke, developing an understanding of their bodies and the responses that are triggered. All these processes are going to come with mistakes and great frustration. However, having this met with frustration or impatience from the one you are looking to for love, support and guidance can have long term effects on a child's dignity and self-worth. Children need a secure environment in which they can experience their feelings and learn to see them as being important and valid, not to be feared. Through these early attempts, show them your trust in them as they explore their growing emotions and the behaviours they generate. Empower children as they play and interact with others by drawing attention to the positive choices they are making. Offer alternatives if need be and begin to establish clear and consistent limits. Guide them with confidence and calm stability where needed and show them that you are always there with kindness and support should things go a little wrong.

Empowering children to make their own choices

If you want a child to be able to make positive decisions without you, they need to recognise and understand what it is they are doing and experience taking ownership of those choices. Children are born with social instincts: to share, to play nice and to be thoughtful about the feelings of others. Your job is simply to encourage the development of these social tendencies that are present from birth. When we offer rewards for behaving nicely, sharing or spontaneously helping, it changes the way children think about these behaviours, overwhelming the subtle intrinsic rewards of being a good friend in this social world and can ultimately block these natural efforts. It is far better to draw a child's attention to how good it feels to help someone, the smile they have put on your face or the fun they had in playing nicely (Figure 6.4).

Figure 6.4: Learning to play together and interact is an intrinsic part of succeeding in this social world.

As they get older you can then talk to them about the choices they have made. While the memory of the incident and its consequences are fresh in their mind, consider the choices they might like to consider next time. Talk about more productive alternatives as you look to recognise and understand what happened. And talk to them about their behaviours and the feelings that prompted them.

When you empower a child to make their own choices, sometimes these choices will have fallout. A big part of nurturing a child's behaviour is in helping them to actively manage this fallout. If toys have been thrown, they need to be picked up. An apology can be requested, however, empathy will not develop for some years yet, neither will an understanding of what that apology means, so often a hug or a handshake can be more forthcoming and heartfelt. By feeling the power of their actions, a child is learning that every choice comes with certain outcomes. Allowing them to feel the impact of these, both the positive and the negative, begins to instil in them a sense of responsibility, ready for more informed decisions next time. So, provided they are not life threatening, morally threatening or unhealthy, give children an active choice about their behaviours, rather than seeking to control their every movement. This is an important step in helping them to understand themselves, as well as teaching them about how the world works.

Managing the influences on children's behaviours

As a child grows and develops, their behaviours will be shaped by what they see around them. So, while this can be shaped by you, it is important that you take these opportunities to teach them about the active choices they can make about how they behave. But when it comes to how you influence these behaviours, you must be careful. We have all seen the sticker chart proudly displayed on the wall, heard the treat being promised, and yet if the children would just help pick up the toys or get ready for lunch another incentive could be found. When that does not seem to be working the frustrations rise, as does the volume, the "time-outs" and the pleading. So, where is it all going wrong?

When you simply tell a child the behaviours you expect, they develop no deeper understanding of why they should behave that way. Nor do they have any real commitment towards what they are doing, beyond fear of losing the promised reward or attention. Any behavioural management tool that looks to control, manipulate or demand compliance does nothing to teach a child. Instead, the actions they are coerced into taking become done purely for the pay off. And in time, the people around them are viewed as obstacles in the way of what they want. All a child learns from this approach is to ask "What is in it for me?" "Are you seeing what I am doing?" And "Am I doing this the right way... I mean your way?" Whilst this may seem on the surface to describe a compliant, "well-behaved" child, at what cost? Do these sound like childhood lessons that will lead to healthy adult relationships?

Children need firstly to understand what is expected of them. And you need to make sure that these expectations are not too much. Are you becoming upset because they are taking too long getting ready to go outside when their fine motor skills are not able to perform the necessary tasks at speed? Are tensions brewing because their bricks are on the floor when they or others around them have done this all week? Or are they hearing exasperated tones for something they did not know was a problem and still do not understand? Their social and emotional development must also be an important consideration when nurturing their developing behaviours. When it comes to the complex processes that surround human interactions and the rules that govern them, mistakes will be made.

- Firstly understand the developmental stage of the child, **not just their age**, as you consider the expectations you are putting on them

- Be mindful of any triggers that might be at play, yours as well as theirs

- Look to be constructive and encouraging as you make it clear what you want

- Talk about what is needed without emotion, leaving you both feeling good about the experience

- Help them to see that their actions will have consequences: "Once the toys are picked up we can go outside".

Through these consistent, sustainable techniques, you are then showing a child that you respect them and that you trust they can take responsibility for their actions. As they experience managing these situations for themselves, they can develop a strong sense of inner discipline that will allow them to choose to behave in responsible and compassionate ways, wherever they may be.

7 Helping children feel competent, confident and worthy

When a child is born, they do not yet have any understanding of what it means to be their own, separate person. They are not yet able to differentiate themselves from their mother. They do not yet know that these hands and feet belong to them and that they are in control of them. They are not aware that they can have their own, independent responses to things, their own feelings or emotions. Nor do they realise that the other people around them can also have their own responses, feelings or emotions that might be different to their own. Developing an individualised sense of being someone different happens over time as a child develops the mental, emotional and behavioural functions necessary to see themselves as a separate person.

Through the enriching experiences they are given, a child effectively begins to take ownership of their own body, managing how they move it and the things they want it to do with it. They learn to respond to the basic needs and drives that their bodies are telling them. And they begin to realise that in many ways these may be different to the other bodies around them. As they develop this sense of being a separate person, their awareness of who they are develops. It is rooted within these experiences and our responses to them that they establish a growing confidence in themselves as a person.

However, children who have experienced limited opportunities or frequently have adults who step in do not have the chance to develop this sense of security within their own abilities. They may feel unsafe within unfamiliar situations, possibly causing them to shy away from new experiences, lacking opportunities to find new areas of ability or strength. It is then key that we support our children as they establish a sense of who they are and what they can do, along with the feelings of competence, confidence and worthiness that come from it.

DOI: 10.4324/9781003327073-8

Knowledge

Know what competence, confidence and worthiness mean during early childhood and the impact they have on a developing child

As our children grow and develop, they are undergoing many processes. Some we can see clearly happening as they learn to walk, say their first words and put their coat on for the first time. Others are more deeply established and often hidden from our eyes. As a child learns to manage their bodies, process their thoughts and meet their basic needs and drives, they are doing more than saving you the job of doing it. They are developing a sense of who they are and what they can do. With this comes a growing sense of their abilities (competence), their belief in themselves (confidence) and whether this is enough to measure up (worthiness). These are a natural part of living within this social world, but if we want to support their development within our children, we must first understand what they are and what they mean.

Competence: The ability to do something successfully

When we speak of competence, it can mean different things to different people. For example, social and emotional competence is rooted in a child's ability to recognise and deal with their emotions, to solve problems and to manage all the expectations of being a good friend. These are mature ideas indeed. In fact, in a court of law a child's competence is only assigned with age. And yet principles of well-known child-development theories are rooted in the belief that all children are competent and capable and must be viewed as active and valuable members of the wider community.

Competence then is all about having the sufficient skills, knowledge or ability to do something in the area we want to be judged competent in. In our society this tends to be associated with age because we tend to judge a person's competence to do something through proof, on demand, that they are able to. This might come from producing their qualifications or a demonstration of them doing it again. However, competence is far more deeply ingrained within us than this.

To have competence in something means being able to do it, and this requires a personal ownership of your actions and their outcomes. When a child is first born they have no understanding that the fuzzy clump that keeps passing before their eyes is actually their own hand, so personal ownership of their actions would be somewhat of a stretch. However, the development of these ideas are already taking root. Given opportunities to cause an outcome, such as making their toy move or to create a noise when they hit out at a rattle, they develop this sense of ownership of their actions. And you will see this beautifully almost as soon as they have their first words, with a particular fondness for the word

'Mine' and the phrase 'Me do it!' This developmental stage demonstrates the emergence of their personality early on as they begin to recognise and take ownership of themselves.

Confidence: Having the belief that you can do something successfully

While being competent is all about your abilities, feeling confident is about your belief in them. And this comes from experiencing your successes (Figure 7.1). Expressed in this way it is clear to see how conditional a child's confidence is on their past experiences. Fuelled by every success and dented when things go wrong, confidence is then all about a child's faith or trust in themselves and where their abilities to do something reside. This is why young children sound so confident when telling you how they will beat you in a race or how they can perform cartwheels well beyond their means. They have not had much experience of not being able to. Their confidence is built through the memories of times they have done things

Figure 7.1: Every time a child experiences their growing success at something, their confidence in their abilities can grow.

with ease, when trying again paid off and the positive outcomes that followed.

However, as a child is learning lots of new skills that they have yet to master, their confidence can be easily dented. This does not mean you should make things easy. If that were the case, what would then happen in the real world when things do go wrong? How will they feel trying something and initially failing before the new skills and abilities are learnt and perfected? Mastering something so that you can do it with ease takes lots of initial failures and mistakes. If we do not keep our youthful confidence in our inevitable ability, why would we keep trying again?

It is then important that you keep this balance. Help children to develop new skills, with the time they need to do so. Rushing their attempts to meet an expected time-frame will do little to nurture their confidence. Instead, make sure to build their resilience as you recognise and celebrate their achievements along the way. This does not mean inflating their developing accomplishments or correcting a less than perfect attempt. The praise a child is given is deeply influential to this process and something that is explored more fully in the second book in this series.

Worthiness: Feeling good enough

Worthiness is rooted in our values; our beliefs about what is good, what is right and what is important and how we ourselves measure up. In every interaction we have with a child we are communicating these values to them, both when we mean to and when we do not.

In these first months of life a baby is already developing a sense of how they fit within this social world. Developing an understanding of the people in it and how important they are to them (Figure 7.2). When they cry, are they worthy of a response? When they make eye contact with you, showing you their brightest smile, are they worthy of receiving your smiles back? Are their early attempts at finding things out, at moving their body and making things happen worthy pursuits? Or, when consistently denied or prevented from doing so, are these sim-

Figure 7.2: When you take an interest in what a child is doing, you show them that their efforts are worthwhile and that they are worthy of your time and attention.

ply not worthy of their efforts? The messages we are then sending to our children in these moments are deeply impactful and we need to be aware of them.

As we show our interest in a child, picking up on their cues and being ready to respond to their needs, we are helping to establish this sense of worthiness within them. As we show an interest in what they are doing, whether it is their attempts at grasping for an object slightly out of reach or the noises they are making as they bang two bricks together, we are showing them their efforts are worthwhile and that their discoveries are valid.

As they get a little older and become more aware of the other children, adults and expectations around them, their sense of worthiness extends from being solely about them to being about how they compare. It is then so important that we are mindful of unhelpful comparisons. "Why can't you be more like the girls?" simply helps a child take an instant and intense dislike to the shining example. This is even worse when the example is an unreasonable ideal, like "Why can't you sit still?" when they need to move their bodies. "Why can't you hurry up?" when their fine and gross motor skills are struggling to put their coat on. "Why can't you play nicely?" when they are working through the complex social demands this requires.

In their first years of life, as children are gaining the foundational experiences that all later experiences are built upon, they need lots of opportunities to see what they can do and prove to themselves that they can do the thing they want to feel confident about. Along with this belief in themselves, they need resilience for when they are less than perfect or when mistakes are made. They need to be surrounded by people who value their efforts, rather than simply their successes. When a child has received these positive experiences, they have the confidence to try again when their abilities are questioned, either by themselves or by others. They are ready and able to embrace the goals that are important to them, viewing mistakes as simply learning opportunities as their range of competences grow. And as their self-esteem flourishes, they grow to feel intrinsically worthy, simply for being them, and ready to take all of life's challenges in their stride.

Understanding

Understand how the experiences a baby is offered and the messages they are given can impact their self-esteem and significantly impact their well-being

It may seem a little strange to consider such grown-up terms in a book that talks of nurturing babies. However, as with so much of a child's development, these dispositions do not simply appear fully formed in our older child; they are rooted in every experience that has come before. If we want our children to embrace a challenge, this work begins when they are very young. To believe that the effort is worth their while, they need to know they are capable of learning, with skills already established to support them as well as finding the motivation to continue, even if others' opinions may differ. All our actions and comments have a bearing on this process and we need to know and understand the impact this is having. Only then can we offer the constructive influences our children need, while avoiding the damage that can so easily be caused through an ill-informed response. Damage that can affect their next attempt and the one after in cumulative ways can have serious long-term effects.

Impacting developing self-esteem

When we encourage a very young child to begin feeding themselves or to take their first steps it is only natural to expect some mess on the floor and a few bumps along the way. We do not expect children to succeed the first time or to do something new with ease. However, as children get a little older and the tasks a little more complex, the messages of encouragement can become somewhat distorted. Instead of mistakes, errors and wrong answers being seen as a part of learning, they can become judged as a lack of ability. Instead of a stage they need to pass through on the way to competency, they become confused with a difficult challenge that should be abandoned.

When you support a child through the early stages of not knowing something, you are doing far more than teaching them a new skill. You are showing them what it means to learn something. Demonstrating how these early stages are simply a step on this journey as they move from feeling at a loss and unsure to knowing and competency. The messages children receive as they experience this transition, especially during these foundational years, are already telling them something about what it means to learn, to try and to persevere, and how capable they are likely to be when they encounter this transition the next time. Children need to learn that these feelings of not knowing should not be feared, that they are simply a process that everyone goes through as they develop competency and mastery that says nothing of the person they are or who they can become.

Competence

Through every experience, children are learning, gathering the knowledge and understanding they need to gain a level of competence across a wide spectrum of emotional, cognitive and physical skills. With lots of different experiences and opportunities to develop, a sense of empowerment can grow, informing the way they behave and respond to others.

- **Developing mental processes** – To think for themselves

- **Developing emotional stability** – Understanding the emotions they are feeling and learning to manage them

- **Developing verbal skills** – Speaking and understanding the words they need to express their thoughts, wants and needs

- **Developing physical skills** – Managing their body and learning to use it effectively.

As you support this natural part of a child's personal growth, you can encourage their thoughts by recognising them. You can support their developing emotions by giving them the words to describe them. Notice their actions as you stop for a moment and draw their attention to the things they are doing. As you connect with them you might like to use phrases such as "Do you see how you just managed to do that? That's because you kept trying". Or "You look really sleepy, I think it is time for your nap, are you feeling tired?" Even long before they have the words to answer you, they are listening to you talk about these things as they begin to associate the terms with their feelings and recognising what this means to them.

Confidence

When children are confident, their belief in their ability to learn and develop new skills grows. As they develop confidence in one thing and then another and then many others, a child moves into a state of self-efficacy as they learn to trust in their abilities and have faith in their capacity to persevere. The more they experience going from not being able to do something to doing it with ease, they will realise that it is all just a learning process, allowing them to take on any challenge and follow their dreams. As you help children to identify and build on their strengths, you can help them to see that even when the going gets tough, they can try harder and dig deeper. As they see their renewed efforts result in even greater success, they experience how, with determination and practice, they can master whatever they set their minds to as true faith in themselves begins.

Building confidence

Resist being too quick to do things for them – Let children see what they can do for themselves

Let them experience mistakes – Learning to face their setbacks with resilience rather than fear

Let them believe they can do it – Experiencing their success allows their self-esteem to grow

Pay attention – Let them see your interest in their journey, not just their success

Build resilience – Self-esteem helps children to cope with the eventual setbacks

When children have developed a confident attitude towards learning from a young age, they are more likely to persevere with tasks, making them more likely to do well both in school and at any activity or goal they set for themselves. And when problems or difficulties do arise, they are more likely to have the faith in themselves and their eventual abilities to make additional effort worthwhile, confronting setbacks head on. They are more likely to make their own decisions and stand up for what they believe in and less likely to give in to peer pressure, recognising the risks that are worth taking.

Worthiness

From the day we meet them, children are surrounded by our actions and words, telling them something about how we feel, how we think and the values we consider important (Figure 7.3). How we respond to a child takes this to a deeper level as these thoughts and feelings become focused on them. When we take our time to engage, looking into their eyes and responding to their actions, we are telling them that they are worthy of our time. When we provide warm, nurturing environments full of new and interesting experiences, we are telling them that they are worthy of our efforts.

As children get a little older and start noticing other places we may direct our attention, this too informs them about the things we consider worthy of our time and efforts. And when it comes to other people, whether they are in the room or not, this is going to be inwardly compared. When we start evaluating or judging someone based on a variable quality – how rich,

Figure 7.3: Every interaction is telling a child something about their place in this social world.

clever, thin, successful, popular they are, the list goes on – this is telling the child something about the worth we attribute to them. Consciously or unconsciously we are informing a child of the values they should look for and those they should aspire to possess. The trouble comes when a child hears this and links it to their own feelings of worthiness.

The trouble with assigning value to these conditional qualities is that it implies we must somehow earn our right to be valued as a person, continually proving ourselves worthy according to the conditions assigned. If our value needs to be earned, it can go up or down and it can even be lost. If we do this to our children, they will begin to feel the need to prove themselves on some endless treadmill. Unsurprisingly, this instils a feeling of anxiousness about who they are and every decision they make, with an obvious impact on their well-being and self-esteem. As this then becomes inextricably linked to ideas of self-respect, value and ultimately self-esteem, we can see how children are asking themselves whether they measure up.

Support

Be supported in offering babies the experiences they need so that they may all feel competent, confident and worthy, now and for all the years to come

As we look deeper at supporting these strands of competence, confidence and worthiness, we need to think about how we view success within them. What does it mean to be competent? How do we inspire confidence in others and how can you support a sense of unquestioning worthiness in the children in your life? When we talk about anything to do with a child's mental health or their emotional well-being, it is not enough to consider all the opportunities we are surrounding them with. The most diverse and enriching experiences imaginable will have no benefit to a child who doesn't feel able to access them. And environments designed to stimulate can only do so when the child's mind is open to the possibility. Along with the physical considerations of how well we nurture children, we need also to consider the underlying messages that we are conveying to them.

In the early days, a child's confidence in themselves is strong. It wouldn't occur to them that they are unable to do something. This is why safety features are so important: a lack of confidence in getting back down is certainly not going to stop them from climbing the flight of stairs. But as their competences grow it is important that we help them retain this self-confidence if we want them to continue to try. Our responses to children as they gain more experiences of trying something new and possibly failing on the way to success tells them so much about the value of their efforts, whether it is worth putting in the additional effort and how worthy they are to succeed.

By supporting your children through these processes they can learn that the early stages of not knowing something are simply a part of learning that they need to pass through on the way to competency. Feeling at a loss and unsure, even when this feeling becomes overwhelming, is just a stage that will pass. These feelings should not be misread as a character fault, a lack of ability or proof of a challenge too great; it is simply a process that everyone goes through as they develop competency and mastery and says nothing of their potential – a lesson we want to give all children long before the school gates.

Competence

As carers and educators we need to encourage a sense of competence in our children, a belief in themselves that they can do what they set their minds to and that it is worth the effort of trying. This cannot be given and certainly not through false praise; it is earned through experience. As you offer these experiences to your children, remember to empathise, guide, support and suggest, but do not take away the journey or their sense of pride in its accomplishment.

■ Allow children to experience a challenge

■ Let them solve their own problems

■ Give them opportunities to realise their own successes

■ Allow them to feel proud in themselves

■ Allow them to see your genuine pride in them.

Over time, as children see the actions that trigger praise, they will internalise your standards, so be careful of what and how you praise. I talk about praise in more detail in the second book in this series, but for now, always look to highlight the things a child is in control of rather than intangible qualities, such as their cleverness or greatness that they do not control. As they get older, children will also look to others for this encouragement and validation, but the need for approval from the ones we love never leaves us, so make sure it is achievable and be mindful of the expectations that you are establishing in them.

Confidence

Children begin to recognise their abilities through the opportunities that allow them to use their mind and body, to overcome challenges and to solve their own problems. This can start early on, such as allowing them to reach for a toy rather than immediately passing it to them (Figure 7.4). As you look to retain a child's

Figure 7.4: When a young child has the opportunity to watch what others can do and then try for themselves, their confidence in their growing capabilities can flourish.

confidence when they become more knowing and aware of their potential for failing, look to build on their strengths. You can then offer experiences that extend the learning process in achievable increments with lots of opportunities to go back and try again.

The self-esteem emerging here can have a positive effect across all areas of learning, so value it, even if it is a little unusual. The need to climb the steps may have lost its appeal to you after the 100th time you have supported them with it, but the learning that is going on is invaluable, teaching them about the muscles in their arms and legs, their balance receptors, the effort needed, even the changing view from the top step. All of these transferable skills are essential to their ongoing development, along with the boost in confidence every day they get a little better at the task.

If a child is lacking in confidence, help them to reflect on their efforts in different ways, "You didn't manage it today... but you got further! Let's see what you can do when you try again tomorrow" or, "You got to the top, that is because you have been working so hard", rather than because they are so strong, so good or so clever. Even before they have the vocabulary to use these terms for themselves, children are taking more meaning from the words and sentiments you use than you may think.

As they get older and more experienced within the environment, allow them to use their past experiences and power of thought to figure things out.

- Set achievable challenges and lots of little things that they can do for themselves

- Place hidden objects for them to find in the places you hid them yesterday

- If they have used fabric to drag a toy toward them, set up the same resources so they can repeat the trick again

- If they are on the verge of accomplishing a new skill, give them lots of opportunities to keep trying

As you offer these experiences, children will discover that they can achieve things for themselves, even if it is different to what you had in mind. So, help them to see that their thoughts and actions can be powerful and influential as they alter their outcomes for themselves.

Worthiness

The feeling of having unconditional value and worth, of being accepted and acknowledged simply for being you, are human rights given to a child from birth. Children don't have to prove anything to be somebody; our job is simply to offer them the freedoms and support to fully express the "somebody" that they want to be. Being a good model of this is critical whenever you are around a young child, along with accepting and valuing the directions they wish to take. To do this effectively, you need to ensure every child feels valued and loved. No matter how busy your environment or how many children you may have in it, ensure you see the innate worthiness of every child.

■ Not every child needs changing at the same time

■ They are not all interested at the same thing in the same moment

■ Some children need a little longer

■ Some will need to revisit

■ Children need to rest when THEY are tired

■ Children develop and grow at their own rate; you can support and encourage but not rush

As you support a child's competencies, confidence and sense of worth, be aware of how they are viewing the environment you offer to them. What do they see and access? How are you supporting their thinking? As you talk with children, consider their thoughts and emotions as you ask them "What do you think about that?" "How would that make you feel?" "What would you like to do?" – even before they have the words to answer you. When we feel included in our lives and a valued part of the community we find ourselves in, our sense of worthiness can flourish. And when we feel optimistic about our abilities and our understanding of the world around us, everything else about our minds and bodies just seems to work much better. We should all aspire to hang onto our childlike optimism for as long and as often as we can. So, look to their example as you model the optimism you would like your children to retain throughout their lives.

8 Empowering resilient children

When we think of resilience, we can often find ourselves thinking of the negative influences that may come into our lives and how equipped we may be to cope with them. However, resilience is an ordinary process that allows us to manage every day and is embedded within a range of character traits and abilities. How well we cope with the more negative influences and situations that we face is therefore a result of our own development; a product of our adaptations to the people and environments we have found ourselves surrounded by and the mechanisms we possess for achieving positive outcomes despite adversity. When these systems have developed well, we should be able to cope even in challenging circumstances. However, if these basic systems have been compromised, the risk for difficulties in our development increases with impacts felt throughout our lives.

Resilience is our capacity to thrive, despite whatever difficult circumstances may come our way. It allows us to overcome adversity, to continue functioning despite challenging circumstances and to rebound after we have experienced trauma. This means very different things to different people, but to a child who can feel powerless at the best of times, their need for resilience becomes even more apparent.

Children, by virtue of their age and dependency, are not able to choose the people in their lives or the environments they find themselves in. For many, being raised in difficult surroundings is a way of life that they cannot change. Children living with the effects of poverty, violence, substance abuse, family breakdown or illness will find their childhood impacted to some degree with their developmental trajectories invariably knocked off course. And yet, whilst one child may encounter a challenge or difficult situation and crumble, for others adversity may be met with relative ease. As they rise above any difficulties and do well in spite of the challenges they face, these children may be considered to be resilient.

However, despite this outward appearance of resilience, to some degree situations such as these will inhibit a child's normal intellectual, social and emotional development,

DOI: 10.4324/9781003327073-9

all of which will interfere with them reaching their full potential as adults. We, as influential factors within their young lives, must do all we can to safeguard them, their development and their future potential.

Knowledge

Know the importance of resilience in our children and how we can encourage it to form

When resilience is studied, it is often quantified by considering the risk factors children are managing. However, this is not a tick list of labels to assign to children with an expected outcome. These are more like probability statements indicating difficulties for a developing child that we need to be aware of. They will also not necessarily occur in isolation, and an accumulation of these risk factors adds to the potential for negative outcomes. These risk factors may be biological, such as congenital defects and low birth weight. They may stem from a mother's lack of nutrition or medical care during pregnancy. Or they may be environmental factors, such as poverty, family conflict or emotional distress in the home. While it is clear that these may well occur together, a healthy child may also find their circumstances change. We must then be aware of risk factors in every child's life if we are to do all we can to support healthy beginnings.

The importance of encouraging resilience

Children are well aware that their safety and well-being is in the hands of others. Unable to provide themselves with the food, warmth and care they need to thrive, their survival is wholly dependent on the adults around them. They cannot afford for those adults to get tired of doing all they can to support and nurture them. They need love despite the fact that they will often get things wrong. And they cannot afford to be abandoned when things get tough, when they make mistakes or experience challenging emotions and behaviours (Figure 8.1).

Through the unconditional love of a nurturing adult and the tenderness and genuine concern for their physical and emotional well-being, strong-rooted attachments can develop. With these firmly in place, a child can grow with confidence, developing the skills they need to take on greater independence and responsibility and a sense of external

Figure 8.1: The love and care you show a child helps them to feel a valued member of the family or community they find themselves in.

strength and support within their lives as they become an active member of their family, their community and the world.

These relationships and attachments with a primary caregiver have been identified as the most significant factors determining whether children feel safe and happy. Whether this is with parents, grandparents, siblings or a key practitioner, through these positive relationships and sense of belonging, a strong and healthy sense of resilience can be established. Wherever they take root, they need to be nurtured and cherished with the knowledge that the resilience building within the child will last a lifetime.

A feeling of being connected to something larger than ourselves is something we all need from time to time; that there are others out there who are looking out for us, who care, who will catch us if we fall. For a child, this comes firstly from you and other members of their family and the trusted adults they have in their lives. As they get older, relationships with their friends and the groups they belong to will add to this external strength and support. This may come from the school or church they attend, clubs they belong to and organisations they are a part of.

Unfortunately, not all children are surrounded by strong, supportive influences. Instead, they may be experiencing a range of difficulties within their young lives such as poverty, family difficulties or illness. The difficulty may be by virtue of their past experiences or a temporary challenge they may find themselves facing. For these children, often labelled as being "at risk of failing to succeed", it is even more important that we work with the other adults around them to establish a strong, safe base for them to return to. If we want to empower our children, we must then give them an environment where they feel valued, where they can think for themselves, to begin to make choices, decisions and yes, mistakes, safe in the knowledge that they are in a secure place.

Developing resilience in all our children

Studies have identified that resilience is a common phenomenon within all of us to some degree. We are all born with an innate capacity for resilience, which is then adapted through our experiences as we use it to develop a sense of who we are. Are we afraid to make our own decisions, despite not knowing the outcome? Can we strive forward with a sense of purpose even though we may fail? Can we make social connections despite initial rejections? Do we look to solve our problems by trying again or are we quick to give up? And how do we perceive the level of risk around us?

The level of resilience we possess will always be context or content specific. This means that we may be resilient when faced with one type of risk yet overcome by something different. However, through our opportunities to experience these things, we are developing this character trait. Within a place of safety, the situations we find ourselves in and the outcomes we experience will allow us to develop a healthy level of resilience, adapting our own level of resistance to future encounters, every time we respond.

Longitudinal studies spanning decades of research have looked at the impact of negative experiences in children's early life and their long-term effects. These studies suggest that between half and two-thirds of children growing up in families with mentally ill, alcoholic, abusive, or criminally involved parents or in poverty-stricken or war-torn communities do overcome the odds and turn a life trajectory of risk into one that manifests "resilience". This shows our biological possibility for growth and development in the presence of negative environmental situations. The difference with resilient people, studies suggest, comes from the protective factors that have been developed along the way, essentially safeguarding us from the negative impact of an identified risk.

Whilst children may be born with an innate capacity for resilience, it is one thing to for a child to be resilient when all is going well; it is quite another to be able to pick themselves up and try again when things do not go to plan straight away. We need to be mindful that mistakes and wrong turns are embraced by children as a very real part of the learning process as they realise that many attempts may be needed on the journey to perfection. On top of this, life is often full of curveballs, difficulties and problems that we did not see coming but that they need to manage.

Understanding

Understand the signs of resilience and the protective factors that promote it

Research on resilience in child development came firstly from wanting to understand and prevent the development of psychopathology or mental disorders. This was done by studying children who seemed to progress well under risky conditions. Scientists then began looking at the processes and regulatory systems required for protective factors associated with resilience. But as the consequences of major threats to children's development became better known, focus moved towards promoting resilience through prevention, intervention and the policies children need from us, recognising the significant change of trajectory in a child's life when these factors were in place.

While risk factors are circumstances that increase the probability of a poor outcome for a child, they are far from an inevitable conclusion. What may result in a negative outcome for one person may be avoided for another. Studies show that the best way we can support children to achieve positive outcomes despite difficult beginnings is to develop resilience. And one of the ways we can promote a child's resilience to risk is through the development of protective factors.

A study at the University of Minnesota looked at the characteristics and circumstances that children require to overcome difficult situations. After four decades of research, looking at adverse circumstances ranging from poverty to war to natural disasters, they revealed several fundamental conditions that allow children to flourish despite having to face difficulties.

- A close attachment to a competent and caring adult

- Effective skills for problem solving, emotion regulation and self-control

- A belief that life has meaning

- The power to obtain what they want or need

Protective factors children demonstrate

When we think about supporting and enhancing a child's resilience, it is important that we stay focused on their strengths rather than any deficit they may be experiencing. When we concentrate on the positive steps that can be put in place, we can understand the impact we can have on their healthy development and potential outcomes, despite the exposure to risks that we may have no influence over. Protective factors are one such way of achieving this. While the resilience a child is developing is likely to be inhibited by any surrounding risk factors, resilience is promoted by the protective factors that surround a child – individually, through the people they are surrounded by and the communities they live in.

The power of these protective factors is illustrated through the range of responses that different children may have to similar situations. Strengthening these protective factors is then something we can tangibly do to optimise a child's resilience, and we can do this through the influence we have on their relationships, environment and community.

- **Relationships** – The positive attachments being formed in a child's early experiences of relationships are key to promoting their resilience. Whether they are spending this time in the care of one parent or experiencing the nurturing care of a range of key people; whether this is experienced in the home or between a range of environments; children need responsive and understanding adults (Figure 8.2). They need to feel protected, nurtured and surrounded by a style of care that is both rational and consistent but not controlling. They need to experience love and support, as well as see positive emotions and supportive interactions being modelled through the relationships around them.

Figure 8.2: Responsive and understanding care offers a child a sense of security. Only when this is in place can they develop the resilience they need for those moments when things may get tough.

- **Environment** – Children need warm, encouraging and supportive environments. They need stimulation as well as the time and space to develop close bonds with their caregivers. Within this environment they need to be able to find their voice and use it, developing their communication skills and social behaviours. They need an environment where they can relax, to safely feel their emotions and experience what it means to provoke positive emotions from those around them.

- **Community** – The environments and social structures children experience outside the family home or care environment can also be potential buffers for children. These are important elements of any effective community, but especially when a child may be at risk. Within an effective community, the presence of stress on a child can be detected early. Before it begins to affect healthy development, steps can be taken to ease a family's exposure to risk, whether through early prevention and intervention programs or by offering a place of safety and the services that are needed. When these community supports are offered within the context of a child's individual culture, they can be especially effective at identifying potential risk and offering the targeted support required to help manage it.

Children surrounded with these protective factors are more likely to be independent, self-sufficient and more confident in their ability to overcome hurdles. With positive self-esteem, they are more likely to make use of the opportunities and resources that are available to them, viewing challenges as a learning experience, with faith that things can work out. As these children encounter a problem, they have the support structures in place to take positive actions or trial different problem-solving techniques. And when they overcome a challenge, their belief in their ability to cope develops. Through the attachments you are forming, the environments you offer and the skills you are allowing a child to develop, you are enhancing their ability to manage during difficult times and to build their resilience with the potential to alter or even reverse the negative outcomes that might otherwise be expected as a result of a child's unavoidable life stressors.

Through the opportunities you give a child to investigate something of interest and participate where they can, you are developing feelings of confidence, strengthening them against future vulnerability. For example, within caring and supportive relationships children can experience what it means to feel attached to someone who is putting their needs first. As they experience your faith and compassion in a place of safety, this drives them towards showing compassion, understanding and respect to others. When you help them to feel a member of the group, you help foster a belief that they are a part of something bigger than themselves, developing the social skills and wider awareness that are essential to their feelings of happiness, security and meaningful participation.

Empowering children's resilience

The impact we have on a child's outcomes through the style of caring used has been well documented since the 17th and 18th centuries. In fact, at the Foundation of

Psychological Science and Developmental Science, philosophers John Locke and Jean Jack Rousseau described children as "blank slates", ready to be shaped by the experiences offered to them. We now know that development is a little more complex; however, the experiences children are offered throughout their early lives are of foundational and lasting importance. Their potential for resilience towards all that life may present to them is a key part of shaping their behaviours and nurturing their development as they mould the person they are going to be.

As we look to empower children, we need to provide a secure, calm, nurturing environment where they feel empowered to try, and where they can make the mistakes they need to be able to learn from them. Could you imagine having a go at something new, knowing you could be penalised or ridiculed for anything you got wrong? How keen would you be to try? And how safe and at ease would you feel? When we empower another person, we can feel that sense of power enrich our own self-esteem as respect and the depth of the relationship flourishes. However, if you are going to empower a child, you need to first feel empowered yourself. There is a reason why you put your own life jacket on before helping anyone else with theirs!

Empowering a child to become a responsible, resilient and compassionate person is a process they undergo throughout their childhood. It involves being able to make judgments for themselves, to be aware of their actions and the consequences of them. And it means taking responsibility for both their accomplishments and their mistakes, something I explore throughout the books in this series. Once this empowerment is in place, however, children are able to make decisions in their own best interest, to stand up for what they want and need and for the rights and needs of others.

Support

Be supported to implement practices that promote resilience and its underpinning characteristics to take root

When you surround a child with your repeated patterns of behaviour, you are instilling in them the idea of organisation and expectation. When this is experienced within positive, nurturing environments, where children receive the care, guidance and necessary support to achieve these expectations and set some of their own, they can really fly. When you allow children a voice and a choice, they can see the power of going for what they want and believe in, realising that they can have an impact on their environment and outcomes. And through these opportunities to participate, children can develop the more executive skills of problem solving, emotion regulation and self-control, along with personal ownership over their actions as they become more responsible and independent in their activities and learning experiences and developing a belief in

The Road to Executive Functioning

Helping children to see the bigger picture

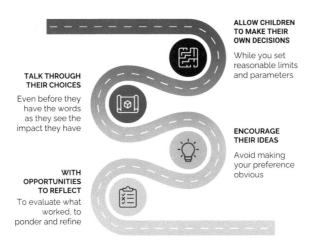

ALLOW CHILDREN TO MAKE THEIR OWN DECISIONS

While you set reasonable limits and parameters

TALK THROUGH THEIR CHOICES

Even before they have the words as they see the impact they have

ENCOURAGE THEIR IDEAS

Avoid making your preference obvious

WITH OPPORTUNITIES TO REFLECT

To evaluate what worked, to ponder and refine

Figure 8.3: The Road to Executive Functioning - The development of executive functions is complex. By helping children experience the consequences of their actions this process is more meaningful and far more effective.

themselves and in their futures, along with the critical resilience traits of self-esteem and self-efficacy, autonomy and optimism (Figure 8.3).

Flexible routine and structure are a great place to start. When children experience being a part of reliable and familiar routines, they are offered a sense of security and stability, especially when you share with them the reasons why things are done in a certain way and offer an element of power that they control. For example, knowing that every afternoon we come together to share some time, some stories and songs. However, if we are absorbed in what we are doing, the timing of our "together time" can wait a little while longer. And on the day the bunny we had been planning for arrived, story and song time could be skipped as we got to know our new friend.

Supporting children as they experience risk

An element of risk is a very real part of everyone's lives. Instead of looking to remove risk from a child's life, we need to think about supporting children to learn to manage it, developing the personal coping skills and resources they need before they encounter more serious issues without you around for support. The ways in which a child copes with stress are also highly dependent on the characteristics they have formed, effectively damping or amplifying the impact of this stress in ways that can have a tremendous bearing on the outcome.

One way of developing these characteristics in children is by introducing them to low levels of risk within a safe environment. There needs to be enough of a risk to represent a challenge, but not enough to result in a feeling of helplessness, so one needs to be tremendously mindful of each child. When pitched at an appropriate level, these experiences of managed stress and the feeling of growing competence that establishes through them can promote resilient attributes. And as children learn to use their growing resources with every exposure to risk, they are learning to overcome it, developing the qualities that allow them to be resilient to risk factors rather than being overcome by them.

Individual characteristics of resilient children

While every child is different, certain characteristics or attributes have been noted in resilient children. By supporting children to develop these attributes we can help safeguard them during more difficult times. To do this, we need to offer repeated, warm and loving experiences, where a sense of familiarity and security can develop as you offer children the protective shields they need now and throughout life's experiences.

Social skills – When children have developed good communication skills, they are better able to establish positive relationships with adults and other children, experiencing what it means to form bonds with those that are close to them, as well as in their wider community. Through these relationships they learn what it means to be responsive to other people and to show a caring, flexible attitude.

- Show your children unconditional love, tenderness and genuine concern

- Develop close attachments within a place of trust as they know "You've got them", no matter what

- Offer them respect rather than the "I am the adult; I know best and you will comply" approach

- Be mindful of their sense of empowerment and resilience as you help them understand not all things are possible

- When you need to tell them they cannot do something, talk about consequences and compromise rather than denial

Problem-solving skills – Children have significant and diverse methods of thinking from a very early age, long before they have the vocabulary to express their ideas clearly. When they can think in the abstract and think critically, creatively and reflectively, they can generate different solutions for problems they may encounter. Given opportunities to plan and be resourceful, they can experience these personal strengths as they learn they can rely on them.

- Support these processes as you help them think of past experiences or encourage them into different areas of the environment

- Be mindful when you set limits and parameters, asking yourself who these are for

- Encourage their interests and motivation when they are wavering, rather than expecting them to follow your lead, which is significantly less satisfying

- Offer potential positive solutions or alternative outcomes and observe the things they try, possibly with new suggestions

- Invite them to make their own decisions and as they get older, talk through their possible actions, the behaviours this might involve and the potential consequences

Critical consciousness – When children are given opportunities to follow their own drives, they develop a greater awareness of what is going on around them, becoming better informed of possibilities and more insightful as they understand their options and what they can do with them. When this is in place, children can develop a greater bank of strategies to overcome any issues they may encounter.

- Offer children opportunities to have ideas and try them out

- Notice when their activities may support others; this offers a huge boost to a child's self-esteem

- Take opportunities to support others in the community, perhaps visiting older generations or an animal shelter

- Encourage small acts of kindness as children learn to establish and maintain meaningful relationships.

Autonomy – When you allow children to act independently, with some control over their environment and choices, they are able to develop a sense of their own identity. They experience what it means to make a choice and the consequences of that choice. They can demonstrate the things they can do to themselves and select their next challenge, seeing their abilities develop (Figure 8.4).

Figure 8.4: Given a sense of autonomy within their environment, independent to engage with who they want and to move and interact freely, children develop a sense of personal agency.

- Offer children the opportunity to have an opinion through the choices they make and the experiences they engage in

- Limit times when children are expected to simply conform to your expectations, and instead let them experience what it means to be an individual from an early age

■ Some structure within your routines can offer children a greater knowledge of what might happen and how, managing these expectations in their own mind

■ As soon as they are old enough, allow them to have their say, verbally and nonverbally as they see their opinions reflected in the actions being taken

■ Offer them some responsibility, for example laying out the mats for an activity or setting out cutlery for lunch as they become familiar with the systematic approach of these tasks

■ Make tidying away their toys a game – the dolls in the blue tub, cars and track in the red tub

A sense of purpose – When children experience setting their own goals, they are more motivated to achieve them. They demonstrate greater persistence and show a more optimistic outlook. When this becomes a familiar experience for them, they develop a belief in the things they can achieve and are far more likely to believe in a brighter future for themselves.

■ Allow children to gain a sense of what they can achieve

■ This does not mean getting it right every time and certainly not the first time they try, so support continued efforts and small wins along the way to a bigger goal

■ Support their developing sense of security within the environment by giving them some control. For example, if everything has a place, children will know where to find things

■ Manage your time so that you are not rushed in the lead-up to transitions

■ Allow children to become more actively involved in the ebb and flow of the day as they see themselves as a contributing, valuable member of the community, group or family unit

9 Supporting children's learning

When we smile into the face of a young baby, it is all too easy to be captivated by the newness of this preverbal, pre-mobile dependent who seems to not be doing very much of lasting value. But we would be wrong to underestimate the immense rate of rapid development that is going on during every moment of these extremely sensitive first years and the impact all this has on their future education.

As you become familiar with the ways a child is growing and developing, your thoughts may turn to how you can best support them in their learning. You may begin to question whether this is more influenced by the genetics they were born with, or the influence you are having on their environment and the experiences you are offering them. This nature versus nurture debate has fuelled long-standing questions in developmental research seeking to understand how much we are influenced by our genetic coding and how much depends on our experiences and the environment we are born into.

Studies in the past have looked at uncovering the greatest positive impact on accelerating children's education and developmental progress. However, I would suggest that a more interesting question is how we can best offer our children a depth of learning as we ignite their passions and interest in the world. After all, how impressed would you be if your surgeon proudly turned to you on the eve of a major operation to exclaim how they had whizzed through medical school at twice the usual speed? Would you not rather they had taken the time needed to do a really thorough job of learning and perfecting their skills, while still retaining a love of what they are doing?

Learning is a complex business that merges both nature and nurture. It combines multifaceted processes that require time and opportunities to be practiced and developed. Influenced through every previous experience, the processes of thinking, learning and developing a child's knowledge need understanding from the very beginning. That also makes the learning process highly personal in ways that can only be achieved when a child has curiosity, autonomy and the opportunities they need. So rather than reaching for another toy catalogue or website for ideas, understand the difference you

DOI: 10.4324/9781003327073-10

can make as you learn to offer enriched, powerful learning experiences from the very beginning.

Knowledge

Know the difference between learning and educating a child, reflecting on this as we harness engagement and refocus our attention in the early years

From the time they are born a baby is inquisitive about their world, especially the humans in it and particularly their faces, as they try everything to engage and interact. In the early months, children are driven to explore, play and investigate their sur-roundings and the objects within their reach before connecting with others and using play to engage and make social con-nections. As they grow and develop, the ways in which a child plays will change, but this foundational way of learning about everything around them will always stay with them (Figure 9.1).

Figure 9.1: Children are learning through every experience they are offered, understanding their environment and the people in it through every sense.

Learning rather than educating

The beauty of thinking about learning, rather than "educating" children, is the intrin-sic diversity and freedom that it suggests. Learning is not confined to prescribed tasks or discrete facts to memorise. Instead, in playful learning, children will naturally engage in math-related activities as they solve problems and rely on patterns and the sequenc-ing of events. Play promotes future writing through the vocabularies that are being developed. As they play games children are developing their social reasoning, physical coordination and artistic and spatial creativity. While a child wants to do this from the moment they are born, external demands, ill-designed toys and the lure of modern technology can get in the way of this process when it is not properly understood and these natural responses can become easily over-ridden.

We all want our children to be good at reading, writing and arithmetic, and have an interest in geography, chemistry, physics and history, believing that skills and knowledge in these areas will lead to academic success and greater choices in their future. However, without the social skills, motivation, enquiry and curiosity fostered during playful learning, we undervalue children's potential in these areas and their interest and engage-ment in the education system is seen to decline. If instead children are surrounded by meaningful experiences, they are naturally drawn to the development of key dispositions of learning. These key dispositions such as curiosity, motivation and intuition will have been formed within powerful learners. These dispositions need identifying, protecting and celebrating as you strengthen a child's early development through the experiences you offer them as a baby, a toddler and in all the years to come.

Play is and will always be every child's most powerful mechanism for understanding the world. It is so interlinked with learning that they are indistinguishable from a child's actions as they embrace both simultaneously. But because direction is given by the child, many parents and teachers are not comfortable or well enough informed to give children the trust they need to succeed using these methods. However, when play is overlooked, children will find ways to include play for themselves, such as using "silly" or "playful" words when they are expected to behave in more constricted ways, fidgeting when asked to sit on the carpet or playing at balancing the chair on two legs.

Promoting engagement

We all learn best when we are pursuing answers to our own questions, seeking knowledge and skills to achieve our personal goals and solve our own immediate problems. This is especially true for children. Deep learning of a meaningful quality is a highly personal process, achieved through repeated explorations of ideas rather than through sequences of steps that will be identical for every child. This cyclical or spiral process must be accessed from where each child needs it as they acquire the next piece of their learning puzzle. But to do this, children need opportunities grounded in experiences of "real life" relevance where instruction is woven through the context of playful activities rather than artificial scenarios planned in advance.

While there are times when children need to learn factual, discrete facts, if we limit children's activities to those chosen for them, where is the enthusiasm, the drive or the passion? When children are closely supervised and controlled, they may learn more of what you want them to in the short term but are shown to learn less overall. And more worryingly, they lose interest in learning, switching off from formal education when it has barely begun. So, I ask you, do you want your children to be the ones who read first or the ones who love reading?

When children are given opportunities to gain understanding through their play, they use these experiences as building blocks for more sophisticated patterns of learning to follow. Through playful experiences of improvisation, interaction and listening to others, children are relating to their surroundings. And as they explore their own ideas and challenge their understanding of concepts, they are gaining a deeper awareness of how the world works and their place within it.

Mindfully considering the principles that guide you

Nurturing children's growth and development can be a daunting prospect – arguably even more so when it is the early childhood of someone else's children that you have such a pivotal role in. When you are caring for a child, you will find yourself needing to make important decisions every moment of every day. What activities and experiences will you offer? How will you interest a child who seems to be anything but interested? What will you do when they want to do one thing, but now is not their scheduled time to do so? Without a framework of informed principles or beliefs to guide your actions you are unlikely to respond with consistency or any degree of conviction. This is just as true as you consider the learning that you believe to be important.

Without careful thought and consideration ahead of time, we can find ourselves reacting to a moment rather than employing a carefully considered approach. Sometimes this may be exactly what a child needs, for example if they have shown an interest in something unexpected. However, with no consideration or reflection you could find yourself falling into automatic behaviours that you know are not great. You may find yourself planning activities when you know they were not overly inspiring the last time you tried them. Or repeating phrases to children as they play, intended to stimulate their learning, yet doing anything but as you wonder why the learning opportunity planned is falling short.

The processes of learning that a child is engaged in from before they are born are complex, interwoven and continual. They will revisit ideas and skills as they assimilate, reflect and adapt, perfecting their understanding as their minds and bodies grow and establishing the dispositions for and attitudes towards all their future learning. Fuelled through every experience and supported through every sense, this is far more complex and important than simply bestowing information or prompting a desired response. If a child is to be able to apply their knowledge and understanding, learning must be about more than displayed abilities or discrete facts to learn (Figure 9.2). It needs to be about concepts that are understood to such a level that they can be adapted and used in other situations. It is about developing a mind capable of thinking for themselves with the motivations and inclinations to do so. All of this starts now, with you, in their early years.

Figure 9.2: Develop a child's learning powers through every opportunity you give them to be inquisitive, to think and explore.

Understanding

Understand the foundations of learning and the importance of nurturing these early stages through the experiences we offer

When we think of a child's learning, our thoughts can soon turn to education and preparations for learning within the classroom. Unfortunately, formal education is increasingly driven by long lists of skills and knowledge that children should possess by a particular age. To fit it all in, choices are made over what is put at the top of those lists and what is left out. And independent exploration and play, even in the very early classrooms, can be left out, despite play being the deepest form of learning that a child experiences. It is then so important that every opportunity you have to lay these foundations in their early years is embraced.

Play is the natural learning instinct and survival mechanism that we are born with. It gives us the desires we need to develop the characteristics of a good learner, to become an empathetic friend and to establish a sense of ourselves. When children play, exploring environments both inside and out, they get to "try the world on for size". Testing their ideas through "I wonder if" or "What if it were" scenarios and developing highly personal ways of understanding as they can begin to make sense of the world and work out their responses to it.

But these core processes need recognising and valuing from the beginning if we are to retain this natural impulse to know and understand, along with the time and opportunities for these complex procedures to establish. Besides, who are we to define what knowledge is more important or what success in the future will look like in this rapidly changing world? Surely, part of childhood is about finding out who you are, what you can do and what a successful future means for you. This speaks of developing children's abilities to learn, rather than seeking to simply educate.

Promoting learning behaviours

In these very early days, one of the clearest demonstrations of the behaviours a child is learning are those centred around food. How they get it, when they get it and what they do when they are offered it. For this reason, looking at babies' behaviour in these moments is a good way of exploring the effects of learning on them.

From the first hours of life a baby is picking up on their internal systems sending them the message that they are hungry and when they have had enough. They turn their head, using the only behaviour they can to let you know, "Thank you for this lovely meal, I have in fact had enough now and do not need any more". Despite this, when a baby spits out their bottle, the tendency is to push it back in until the intended volume has been consumed. When they're a little older, you may yourself remember some coercive practices that you experienced as a child, like being persuaded to "clear your plate", to have "five more mouthfuls" or being told that there would be no sweet reward if you leave the food that has been prepared for you. The trouble is, not only do these methods rarely work in the long run, but they are also actually doing more harm than good.

When we are pressured to do anything, the odds are we will become significantly less likely to want to do it in the future. Worse, in these moments we are overriding the messages children themselves are picking up on. Children are born with all the natural instincts to want to know and understand. If instead of teaching them to embrace these feelings we are in fact expecting them to conform, essentially telling them to ignore the messages their bodies are giving them, the only thing they are learning is that their natural instincts are somehow wrong.

When a child is indicating with every method they have at their disposal that they want to move their bodies, we need to be mindful of our expectations that they sit still. When they reach out, wanting to touch and explore, we need to respect these instincts and nurture them. When they are telling us that they have had enough of the activity we had planned, we must listen. These are their early responses to the learning environments they are experiencing, and we want to encourage them. We want them to realise that they have the power to investigate and see for themselves. When they are compelled to explore, we want to make this a positive experience that they choose to go back to. When their bodies are telling them they need to move, we want them to be able to do so, to hear and respect these messages as they learn to listen to their own bodies and be ready to stand up for what they want in the years to come.

The foundations of complex learning

Unlike surface knowledge, a child's meaningful understanding of something needs opportunities to experience it. Take understanding how weight works for example; how something can be heavier or lighter than something else and what this might tell us about what is inside. When we give babies different things to play with, they are experiencing its weight and the different effort they need to move or lift it. As they get a little older and begin playing with jugs in the water tray or bath, repeatedly emptying the water from them, they are experiencing how its weight changes as it empties. When they then apply this developing idea to a bucket of sand or a bag of feathers, transporting and pouring from different vessels, they are learning to apply familiar concepts to new situations.

Playing with these principles and their underlying understanding of how the world works allows children to gain a deeper awareness of what is happening. In future, this understanding will allow them to know things without needing to experience them first hand. Skills that will inform visualisation and reflection are an integral part of classroom-based learning. But they need to make connections within their learning as they add an increasingly complex structure to their understanding. This requires experiences, lots of them, using their whole body (Figure 9.3).

The ability to learn is a skill like any other. It's a multilayered process combining cognitive, linguistic, perceptual and motor skills in a multitude of formal and informal ways. Developed through every experience, this highly personal journey needs a child to try things for themselves; to take risks and solve problems; to experience the riches

Figure 9.3: A child is learning throughout their whole body, which is why experiences like this are so enjoyable!

of a three-dimensional world, touching, handling and trialling; and to do this within a variety of social encounters. When we give our children opportunities to do all these things, while at the same time engaging with other children and adults, perhaps within wide-ranging social and environmental situations, these skills are allowed to flourish.

Understand the importance of GIFTED Learning

It is all too easy to underestimate the impact our words and responses can have on a child especially when responding to a preverbal one. It is widely acknowledged that we communicate through far more than the words we say and for a baby who does not have the benefit of words, this is especially true. The messages we are then communicating to a baby through our tone, the time we take with them, even our body position is hugely influential. How we encourage their ongoing efforts is a big example of this.

The trouble is, when we get busy we can miss all of these golden opportunities that are too easily taken for granted. With one eye on the clock and the other on the list of tasks we have to get through, we can miss the amazing learning that is going on throughout a young child's day. An infant's brain is growing and developing every moment as they learn from their surroundings – at the same time learning about what it means to learn. When they stretch towards an item just out of reach they are being taught about motivation and persistence. As they splash in the water, or the pureed carrot left over from lunch, they are experiencing cause and effect as they reflect on the impact of their actions. As they investigate the toy under the blanket or the leaves in the tree, they are becoming inquisitive. When we are too quick to pass them their teddy bear, to clean up the spill or to rush past the trees on our way back inside we are missing these rich learning moments.

As your children engage with the world, be sure to observe what they are doing and your own reactions to it. Whether this is from the comfort of your arms as they gaze around the room or are sat playing with a few toys on the carpet. Consider your facial expressions and the encouragements you offer. And think about the time you spend with them, exploring the things that they are attracted to. When you show a genuine interest in what they are doing, taking their lead, you are validating their efforts and their instincts for learning. With your open expression and smiles you are sending positive messages to endorse their natural impulses. And as you learn from this experience together, you are showing them that this is worth their time and effort as clearly it is worthy of yours.

During these moments, we are facilitating children's earliest experiences of the learning process, during which children are experiencing what it means to be curious, to make independent choices and to think for themselves, essentially flexing those dispositional muscles, provided they are given opportunities to engage them. At this point I would like to introduce you to the concept of GIFTED Learning and its importance to lifelong trajectories. GIFTED Learning, or the *Greater Involvement Facilitated Through Engaging in Dispositions*, is the first stage of the Theory of Lifelong Development (ToLD), which we will revisit throughout this series of books.

GIFTED Learning allows our children to become more involved in the learning process when they have had the experiences, the environments and the autonomy to both engage in and develop their dispositional tendencies in positive ways. When this goes well and their efforts are rewarded, a child's tendencies to act in similar ways next time will be encouraged. As they become more confident, curious and intuitive in their approaches, they are more likely to utilise these dispositions, gaining more practice and our engaged young learners flourish (Figure 9.4).

However, if instead they are met with constant direction, distraction or a lack of opportunity for dispositional engagement, this process can become disrupted and our children can quickly become disengaged and reluctant to put in the efforts required. With our every experience informing our next, this process starts very early and these negative impacts become more difficult to reverse with every uninformed experience.

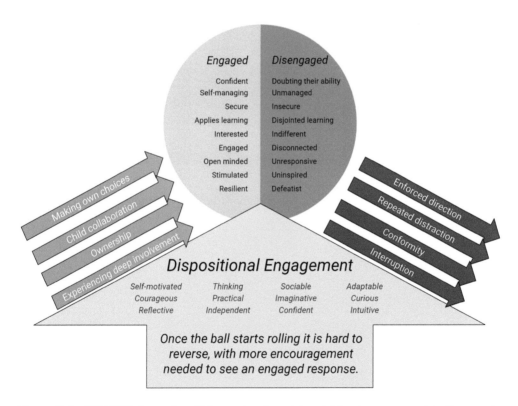

GIFTED Learning
Greater Involvement Facilitated Through Engaging in Dispositions

Figure 9.4: GIFTED Learning This speaks of retaining children's engagement in the learning process and asks you to notice what happens to a child when you take their potential for engagement away.

Support

Be supported in celebrating and validating early learning from day one, recognising the experiences children need

The most important thing you can do to encourage and promote highly successful educational outcomes in the future is to help children to see the wonder of learning. Give them opportunities to discover and learn things about the world and themselves. When you combine this with opportunities to develop their lifelong learning dispositions, children will engage because they want to, not because they have to.

When children are given opportunities to use and combine their newly acquired skills and abilities, they are continuously learning how to perfect them, to arrive at answers that are meaningful to them and to understand what new abilities they need to explore next. But so much more than this, they are learning about their own abilities as a learner, something that they will take with them into every new experience going forward.

By allowing our children opportunities to do things for themselves, to feel what their bodies can do, a sense of personal ownership develops. By providing opportunities to feel a sense of belonging within their environment you allow a child to make sense of their experiences. And by selecting their own goals, they begin to develop a sense of personal power, fuelling feelings of self-esteem and resilience through every experience. But to harness this powerful learning medium and the deeper understanding offered through it, the importance of a child's experiential style of learning must be recognised – especially before the demands of more formal classrooms replace early years environments that are more naturally drenched in play.

Supporting children to experience learning

When children are given opportunities to experience learning first hand, they can experience what they are capable of. As they see what it means to persevere through a challenge, they establish a belief in themselves, becoming more likely to try new things and bounce back quickly when they do experience a failure or setback, developing a good sense of who they are.

With every experience you have with your children, from the first nappy change in the morning to writing their masterpiece in the afternoon, consider how you can maximise the potential of this experience for them no matter how mundane this moment may seem to you or how often it has been repeated. Consider how you can make it open-ended; how you can utilise all their senses. Even something as familiar as a well-loved story can come to life when you think of the sensory learning you can add to it.

Supporting play-based learning

Children have no hesitancy in freely initiating or valuing the learning potential of play. When you offer them open-ended, natural resources in spaces where they feel a sense of ownership, their natural explorations will see them encouraged into new areas of knowledge and challenge. They will find their own way to experience pattern and problem solving. They will take advantage of experiences to combine, transport, adapt and utilise objects freely within their play.

Through whole-body physical movement, they will develop muscle recall, strength and balance. By playing with real objects and materials, links will be made with what is familiar, making connections in their thinking and using greater levels of purposeful vocabulary. Water, sand or mud play explores cause and effect, establishing relationships between actions and consequences. Experimentation, trial and error, inventiveness and risk taking where there is no wrong answer establishes resilience, persistence and curiosity within safe boundaries. Opportunities to reflect on their ideas, to think, consider, ponder and come back to as they need allows them to experiment with ideas before committing them as fact, all the while allowing misconceptions to become evident, allowing you to tactfully guide them.

Supporting children's use of time

Children, especially very young children, are not driven by long-term goals, but rather questions occurring to them here and now. As such they need freedom to respond to whatever is driving them in the moment. With a limit to how much information they can keep in their mind, interruptions can derail a great learning experience. And with their need to allow ideas to germinate, be sure to keep time restrictions at a minimum, with lots of diverse opportunities to get stuck in.

Whilst routines are important for stability and the natural rhythms of the day, take care not to invade their experiences. While having a snack together offers wonderful opportunities for communication, self-expression and engagement, let these occur naturally rather than as enforced breaks from enquiries about to be solved. Observe children as you find a natural break, rather than because it is 10 o'clock, and make sure they have lots of opportunities to return to what they were doing.

Supporting appropriate management

It can become easy to focus on how you are told a child will learn best, undoubtedly through a product someone is trying to sell you or a new initiative that is being launched. What children need, especially in these first years, is to be allowed to experience their success. They need opportunities to try; to establish a secure sense of confidence in their abilities with the strength to meet and succeed in future endeavours. They need experience of making self-initiated and sustained choices through challenging, active learning opportunities where perseverance is rewarded.

However, these ideals can become misguided when an adult agenda gets in the way of a child's independent thinking. Instead, offer children appropriate challenges and risk; limit any activity that tends to dominate their attention, such as the use of a screen. Allow them space for free movement and quiet reflection as they explore the environment, revisiting and embedding concepts with developing self-sufficiency. Be on hand to promote their inquiries but avoid being too quick to intervene; instead, let them manage their own problems. If difficulties arise, support if need be but resist getting too involved or looking to solve problems for them.

Supporting social learning

Only 10% of our communication comes from anything verbal, so from these preverbal days take advantage of all the rich communication that is occurring. From their first interactions with you they will be looking to make eye contact, flailing their arms and legs as they struggle to gain your attention. When a little older they will use smiles to draw you in, even noises designed to attract and keep your attention. As you engage with them, they will be watching you intensely, gazing into your face, watching as your lips move, even copying you if you poke out your tongue or make an "O" shape with your mouth. When a child gets to experience a shared learning moment, the joint feeling of motivation brings with it a bond that cements relationships. Adding a personal sense of involvement promotes their ideas of what they can achieve.

To support these experiences further, offer children the resources they need to engage in meaningful tasks with other children, of different ages when possible. Through the ideas and opportunities you offer, allow them to solve real problems, such as finding out what noise different items will make when banged together, what objects can fit inside the orange tub or how they can grasp a teddy that is just out of reach. Playing with other children, they will watch their ideas and become inspired by them. Give them the time they need to try things for themselves, for as long as they have an interest in it. And when these resources have become less interesting, promote their shared learning with something new, knowing that through this level of deep engagement, you are supporting their mental abilities to flourish.

10 Nurturing lifelong learning with babies

When we talk of learning in the early years, focus can often turn to the preparations needed for the school classroom, almost as if children in their early years are simply preparing for when the important stuff is ready to happen. However, as we saw in the last chapter, the minds and bodies of children during this time are undergoing tremendously formative processes, developing in ways that will have a profound impact on a child for the rest of their life.

With the foundations of effective development establishing future trajectories from day one, it is no wonder that you may find yourself bombarded with every toy, resource and programme essential to giving your children every advantage. Just the thing to promote early literacy skills, an aptitude for mathematical thinking or that elusive "school readiness"! But just how essential are these?

The truth of it is that the features of lifelong learning and a child's dispositions towards them are present in every child and they do need nurturing during these early days. But this requires understanding… not purchasing. And this begins from day one.

For a child doing all they can to understand how this complex and fascinating world works, early experiences of the world deeply impact their learning potential, determining their success at school and their future life trajectories, as well as their health and well-being more profoundly than any other factor. Given opportunities to explore, their instinctive urges to know and understand will intensify. Every time they are encouraged to see something new, to hear an unusual sound, to touch or taste the unfamiliar, their learning processes are stimulated. Memories and pathways essential to their future learning are embedded with every opportunity they are given to think, to feel or to cause a response.

When these experiences are lacking, future opportunities for learning and development are affected. If these endeavours are devalued or continuously interrupted, children will learn that these attempts are simply not worth their efforts. Equally, if they become overstimulated and overwhelmed a child will be quick to retreat, no longer able

DOI: 10.4324/9781003327073-11

to function well. Luckily, they are very good at demonstrating when the experiences you are offering are unmatched to their needs. And with a little knowledge and understanding, you can support and guide them as their features of lifelong learning, their dispositions, flourish. In this chapter we will then consider how processes of development are embedded in every learning opportunity and the difference you can make, through the experiences you offer from day one, to affect a lifetime of learning.

Knowledge

Know how children learn in the first years of life, the experiences this learning depends on and the attachments and sense of security that are needed

So let us start back at the beginning. In Chapter 1, *Good practices from the start*, we spoke about how children's brains are developing from before birth. But let us look at this idea a little deeper. Born with as many brain cells, or neurons, as an adult, the brain will double in size during its first year. So where does this growth come from? It is actually the synapses, the microscopic connections between the neurons, where this growth and development primarily takes place, controlling how the neurons interact with each other and informing a child in the ways they will think and how they will move and behave.

The process of establishing and mapping out these connections is a complex process but can be thought of like taking a stroll through a field of corn. During that first unmapped walk we etch out our unique path. Trodden and flattened by our actions, this will have little effect if we never take the route again; the corn will soon recover as if we never passed through. In the brain, this process is known as pruning and is one of the reasons why we have very few memories from our early childhood. However, if this shortcut proves to be enjoyable or beneficial and we repeat it, the path will become more pronounced and defined with every visit until such time as its permanence no longer needs us. The path will remain, even if we don't walk it for years.

What this means for the infant brain

From birth, the infant brain has 50 trillion synapses firing and making connections through every experience the newborn has. As each of their 100 billion neurons (brain cells) establish more connections, these synapses increase from around 2,500 per neuron at birth to 15,000 by the toddler years. As this growth occurs, this amazing organ is then being constructed and fine-tuned as a quadrillion synapses facilitate the rapid growth and development that is taking effect throughout the body, becoming stronger and more permanent with every engagement. You can see why we are hardwired to seek out new experiences!

Through these experiences, cumulative and explosive processes are establishing and reinforcing the child's visual, auditory and kinaesthetic neural networks, all of which are essential to future learning, while at the same time strengthening muscles and developing a child's internal systems. The engagements offered during this time are then intensely powerful and influential within this process.

While these experiences are being processed across multiple regions of the brain, they are received by information bombarding the child's senses. So, when we offer children experiences that involve multiple senses, we effectively widen this range of stimulation and the potential for learning becomes deeper and more effective. However, in today's fast-paced, modern living, some babies can receive a limited array of sensory stimulation. Separated from the ebb and flow of daily life, they may spend excessive periods of time secured in a chair or, alarmingly, placed in front of a screen. For many reasons, screens with young babies should always be avoided, but most significantly because of all the opportunities this effective pull on their attention is denying them.

Consider for a moment what a child can see and hear when they are left in a sedentary position. Their position and balance receptors are not being activated. Verbal and nonverbal exchanges are not being witnessed or practiced. And as they miss out on experiencing the complete range of sounds, sights and movements required for healthy growth and development, consider the finite number of waking hours they have before this transformative period of growth is complete.

The impact of experience

Throughout this book and the others in the series, you will become aware of just how important the experiences are that we offer to our children and the difference we make to their growth and development through the environments we offer, the opportunities we give for social interactions and the senses we stimulate (Figure 10.1). You'll learn just how important it is that we understand and are able to tune in to a child's moods and their physical comfort as well as their future potential needs and their necessity for responsive and emotive attention as you become mindful of the emotional, intellectual and physical developments that the relationships and environments you offer are fuelling.

From the time they are born, children are learning from and responding to the quality of the relationships and opportunities they are surrounded with. They are highly reliant on the actions and environments they are exposed to, needing wide-ranging and diverse opportunities if they are to effectively construct their rapidly

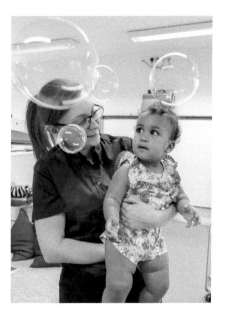

Figure 10.1: Even the simplest of experiences can be all absorbing when experienced by a young child noticing everything for the first time.

developing brain. But more than this, the impact of these experiences and interactions and the ways in which a child is responded to develops the mental pathways that will inform all their future responses such as how they react to external influences, including authority and peer pressure, as well as informing their expectations and perceptions of the world and effectively underpinning the stability of their mental health and well-being.

Surrounded by empathy and love, children are equipped to empathise with others and form meaningful connections. Experiencing appropriately managed levels of everyday stress, they learn to regulate their emotions. Seeing their instinctive attempts at learning met with support and encouragement fosters their love of learning as their mental and physical health flourish. As one experience informs how we respond to the next, all future learning and development is impacted, setting the foundations for the rest of their life.

The social learner

Your interactions are teaching children so much about communication, emotion, feelings and behaviours long before a child has the words to express any of it. Deeply linked to their developing social skills, motivations and behaviours, as well as their belief in themselves, this is where the foundations of lifelong learning are taking root.

The quality relationships and attachments you are forming through your engagements during these early months are so important. Coupled with effective opportunities that allow children to engage with their surroundings, you are teaching them so much about their world and their expectations of it. When they experience responsive, warm and consistent nurturing and care, a child becomes deeply attached to those who are giving it and are ready to respond to every opportunity. You will see this through their physical displays of joy at first seeing you, kicking their arms and legs in exaggerated gestures. They will use animated smiles and facial expressions to connect with you, seeking to reinforce these social bonds.

When these are reciprocated with warmth and openness, their understanding of social behaviours flourishes. However, if these attempts are met with distant, disinterested or closed-off responses, the child will quickly become upset. They will notice straight away and react almost immediately, renewing their efforts with even more vigour as they try desperately to re-engage through every means possible before becoming obviously stressed. So, as you engage with your youngest children, take care not to lose their eager attempts at learning by not recognising or valuing their efforts.

There are of course certain behaviours that you would like to encourage, but remember that a child's behaviours are heavily influenced by their role models and at this young age, this is probably you. So when it comes to learning and new experiences, be sure to display your enthusiasm. Even if this means going outside when you would rather stay in. Or investigating the insects who might be living under the rock. When a child sees you keen to explore and investigate, they will want to mimic you and do the same.

When children naturally go through periods of being reluctant to engage, avoid forcing their efforts or making a big deal of it. The last thing you want to ingrain and reinforce are the learnt behaviours surrounding the idea that "I don't like playing outside" or "I don't like creepy crawlies!" So, be mindful of this before they become unhealthy established behaviours and a lifelong practice.

Understanding

Understand the importance of every moment in these first years, with particular attention to their developing communication and social skills

We think of children developing through milestones. While the timing may vary, we imagine that they hit these developmental stages in basically the same ways and in the same order. However, it is truer to say that necessity is more often the mother of invention; a child will learn what they have an interest in and a need for.

If there was never a need to communicate, if no one spoke to them, would a child bother putting in the effort? Alternatively, when a child is immersed in a world rich in communication and the complexities of language, they will find that their facial expressions alone soon become insufficient and frustrating. As they experience their meaning being misunderstood, children realise that they need to invest in more mature techniques. Within stimulating environments, a child will begin imitating the sounds, patterns and rhythms all around; this starts incredibly early. Researchers have even been able to identify the nationality of a child from the accent of their cry within the first week of life!

Early forms of communication

When you think of a child's earliest forms of communication, you probably think of crying. This is indeed a baby's most effective and immediate means of letting you know they need something. As with all parenting and childcare decisions, this comes with a wealth of advice on how you should respond. We've previously looked at crying when we considered self-soothing during sleep and when we looked at how children express their emotions. But here I would like to consider crying as the simplest form of reaching out and communicating with you.

When thought of in these terms, crying can be seen as something far more significant than a baby demanding attention or getting their needs met. When a baby cries, they are effectively telling you that something does not feel right. They are fully aware that they are powerless to do anything about it on their own and with that comes huge feelings of insecurity and vulnerability. For this reason, ignoring their increasingly upset cries will naturally feel like you are going against your basic instincts. If a three-year-old ran into your arms crying, you would respond; if a friend came to you upset you would seek to find out why. And at these ages they have other options available, a luxury a pre-verbal infant does not have.

When you pick them up and soothe them, you are teaching them that someone is there for them. A someone that cares for and loves them, establishing the roots of attachment that will flourish as your relationship grows. When you do something to rectify the issue, addressing their needs, you are letting them know that they are not completely powerless, but valued and secure. As you show them that they are worth your time and efforts, you actively lay the groundwork for trust, respect and open communication that forms the basis of your ongoing relationship. This early experience of what a reciprocal relationship can and should mean will be reflected in their future expectations.

Developing verbal communication and memory

As we saw in Chapter 1, this preverbal year is an essential period for a child's developing communication skills. As they learn how this complex method of communication works, they will begin developing and fine-tuning the skills and abilities they need to effectively use it. But effective communication is about more than saying the words (Figure 10.2). When we engage with another person, we use a sequence of alternate listening and responding interactions. As we saw, this is imitated by babies in their earliest babbles, in what has been termed a "serve and return" process.

Figure 10.2: A child growing up in a communication rich environment, where they can hear the nuances of speech and are listed to when they respond will experience huge advantages throughout their learning.

In time and with practice, children will embed words and phrases into their babbles. Beginning with familiar objects and routines, this will develop over time to display a deeper understanding of meaning and contexts. But speech needs lots of modelling and practicing, so be aware of the sounds and opportunities that you give children. As you do, embed words and phrases within meaningful contexts, familiar objects and routines as you practise continually. Be mindful of the child who does not seem to be babbling much, but rest assured, they will be taking it all in. After all, there is nothing to suggest that those with the most utterances are the most competent.

Although babies have little in the way of verbal memory, they do have some memory function from birth. This means that, although they are unlikely to remember much of what you say, you can see evidence of this memory in the things that they do. You will see this in their piqued interest over a new toy or how they respond when they see their bib at lunch time. Researchers showing babies at six months old how to light up a toy have observed them remembering how 24 hours later. By two years of age, children can learn nursery rhymes and songs, some of which stay with us for many years to come. As they grow, a child's increasing "learning power" sees them become increasingly interested in the world around them. When we focus our efforts on helping children to gain new experiences, we can help them to feel what it means to try to learn by exploring this deep-felt learning, as well as simply mastering new skills.

Making the most of every experience

When we allow children to explore their curiosities, they actively and automatically engage with the people and environments around them. Provided we are mindful of frustration, we can offer babies achievable challenges that stretch their abilities and encourage their independence and investigation. When we offer an environment that they can touch, manipulate and adapt, children grow in confidence. And as they become more mobile, we can encourage them to ponder and revisit as we avoid doing things for them that they are on the verge of doing for themselves (Figure 10.3). As they learn, their ideas become strengthened and enforced or challenged and dismissed through every experience. And when their senses are stimulated, this neurological development becomes more intense.

Figure 10.3: Young children take in so much from everything around them, making deep connections in their learning, so be sure to offer them as much access as you can.

Children are so keen to accumulate all these experiences because they are such a rich method of learning. Every experience is being received through their senses, so children are most stimulated through novel experiences that utilise them, especially when multiple senses are combined. Through these experiences, the brain is learning to process the information it is given. We have become so good at this that we can interpret new situations we have not experienced before. Our brain can even know more than the raw bits of data we offer it as it goes ahead and fills in the gaps. You can look at a two-dimensional image of a building and imagine yourself moving through it. You can read the words on a menu and conjure feelings, smells, even tastes to mind as your brain draws on past experiences. Even if you have never tried the dish being described in the menu, you will have a good idea of how it will taste, enough to make your mouth water. But to get this good has taken years of enriched opportunities.

However, whilst children need to engage in enriching experiences, there is no evidence that "super enrichment" leads to "super development". So, avoid seeking out ways of doing this, as it is totally unnecessary. Simply think of the experiences you are offering as they engage with their world and consider how their senses are being utilised. How interesting is another plastic toy when they could be holding a feather or crunching some cornflakes underfoot? What are they looking at right now, how about laying under a tree to watch the movement of the leaves in the wind? And be aware of how your children are communicating with you as you enjoy the rich and diverse opportunities all around and the fun things you can be doing together.

Support

Be supported in implementing the foundations of lifelong learning with babies and helping all the key adults in their life to do the same

In the last chapter I spoke to you about the importance of GIFTED learning and how we can facilitate our children's greater involvement in the learning process when we understand and enable the development of the dispositions that are fundamental to it. This may sound complex and involve terms you may not be familiar with, but as you continue reading through this book and the others in the series, you will recognise all of this. Not only in your children, but in yourself… after all, lifelong learning doesn't stop because you leave formal education.

I make no apologies for its multilayered complexity; children are complex. They are continuously learning and developing, in ways that cannot be neatly split into "learning areas" or "focused" activities. They are affected by their environment, the people in it and the autonomy they are offered as they look to engage and try things for themselves, and they are informed by all the experiences that have gone before. This does mean that we need to start straight away, with the experiences we offer from the first time we meet a child. There is much to consider. But through these books I will offer everything you need to nurture GIFTED learning for all your children, now and throughout a lifetime of learning. Exciting, right?

We will look at the ABCs of Developing Engagement (ABCoDE), the Nurturing Childhoods Pedagogical Framework (NCPF), the OPTED Scale that allows you to understand what you are seeing at a deeper level and ways of tracking the impact of your decisions on all of these processes. But to close this chapter and Section One of this first book, I would like to reflect on the specific needs of your babies as you nurture dispositional learning through these first months.

Children need opportunities to fully engage from day one

Children, especially in their very early years, are amazing bundles of possibility. But they are also highly dependent on the adults and opportunities around them. Whilst babies are capable of great learning, their minds and bodies need stimulating. Without the permission and facilitation of the adults around them, this potential is squandered, and frustrated children learn only not to bother.

Children need you to recognise their drives, their emotions and their behaviours. As they look to maximise their opportunities, they cannot do this without the support of a trusted adult providing them with deep and meaningful explorations of all that their world has to offer, guiding them as they translate all the rich detail around them into appropriate responses. But they cannot do this alone. So, if you are not doing so already, let us take a look at some of the small yet significant differences you can introduce to your routines and practices from day one to have significant long-term impacts on children – impacts that will continue to take effect for generations to come.

- Firstly, balance the security of routines and structure with child-led opportunities and freedoms

- Then relax, allowing yourselves time to experiment and explore, rather than correct or follow

- Let children discover at their own pace and see that their interest is important enough to be worthy of your time

- Use open-ended resources and objects that allow children to explore and experiment with their own ideas, with the freedom and time to do so

- As they explore, also appreciate their moments of reflection as they engage, leave and return, rehearsing, reinforcing and refining their understanding

Know the importance of every engagement and interaction

As you spend time with your children, be careful not to dampen their motivations. At this age they are learning so much about their desire to learn. So, whilst they will be compelled to reach out and explore, remember that when these desires are met with disapproval, you are teaching a child not to bother or that these natural instincts are somehow wrong. Alternatively, when you offer them varied opportunities within a rich and engaging environment, you are stimulating deep and powerful learning, triggering connections deep within their brain and supporting development throughout their bodies (Figure 10.4).

Figure 10.4: Even something as simple as sharing a book together can be a magical experience when you consider the sensory experiences you are offering, the moment of connection and the feelings of trust and expectation that are forming.

For example, do you know that how well a child can manage to sit at a school desk, without fidgeting and with enough comfort to concentrate on the lesson, begins with the "tummy time" they receive as a baby? That their vocabulary upon starting school will depend heavily on how well they are communicated with from birth, with the opportunity of hearing tens of millions more words in a communication-rich environment than one where this is not a feature? And that the ease with which they take to reading and spelling will depend on the moments of quietness in their early years when they were given the opportunity to hear subtle differences in sound?

Most importantly, ensure that your children have emotional stability. Children need you to understand their internal drivers and to teach them how to manage their motivations. They need your permission and understanding as they investigate and manipulate their environment just to see what will happen. When all of this is happening within loving and secure relationships, they can then turn their attention to all their other pursuits.

The damage that is otherwise done

Children need a childhood to grow and develop in all the ways that are essential to a lifetime of learning and enquiry. Unfortunately, there is an intruder invading this time of free movement and exploration. From the smartphone in our pocket to in-car players, children are continuously exposed to video screens. With media companies working aggressively to ensure you never need to switch programs, these are intentionally captivating. Screens have become a way of life in most homes and out of them, so much so that their use often goes unquestioned or unmonitored.

When you look at the increasingly lower ages that children are put in front of screens and even offered one of their very own, it is easy to see how this is becoming an unquestioned habit. We come into a room and automatically pop the TV or music on; there is nothing particularly worth listening to, but there it is, constantly playing. And when we are away from the house, within minutes we are reaching for the screen in our pocket. The trouble with this passive, background exposure to media is that it can grab and hold the attention of adults and children alike, meaning interactions and communication is reduced, and for young children in the process of learning social skills, this is bad news. With it becoming such an integral part of everyone's life, it takes a lot of courage to question it, but these issues must be raised.

- Constant exposure to media stops a young child from tuning in to the nuances of speech and discourages or prevents any form of the feedback that is vital to their developing vocabulary

- The more time a child watches television, the more negatively their vocabulary and cognitive development are impacted

- Without the need for human interaction, children avoid needing to develop social skills

- The effects of constant background media are repeatedly reflected in tests of children's cognitive skills and executive functions

Children have a finite number of waking hours during these first years in which to develop an array of skills. Why would you waste a minute of them?

Section 2

Introduction

The Nurturing Childhoods Pedagogical Framework

The Nurturing Childhoods Pedagogical Framework

In previous chapters I have spoken about the importance of GIFTED learning and how we can facilitate our children's greater involvement in the learning process when we understand and enable our children's engagement in the dispositions that are fundamental to it. We have explored how this is a complex process; that it is holistic, continuous and deeply rooted in the moment; and how it is affected by the child, the environment and its permissions alongside the knowledge and understanding of every adult gatekeeper governing it. To that end these books are written to nurture your knowledge and understanding of these holistic facets of child development and to support you as you nurture the children in your life.

As we now turn our attentions to applying these principles in practice, I would firstly like to introduce you to the Nurturing Childhoods Pedagogical Framework. In future books in this series, as we turn our attention to more mobile children with greater autonomy, I will add the ABCs of Developing Engagement (ABCoDE) to this framework. As we consider children with a few more years of learning experiences behind them, I will also add methods that will allow you to look at the impact these experiences are having on your children. And as we turn our attention to practices within more formalised environments, I will introduce you to techniques that demonstrate the impact of a range of variables on a child's engaged experiences. But first let us take a look at the Nurturing Childhoods Pedagogical Framework, as represented by the Framework Flower.

The first thing to notice is that the Nurturing Childhoods Pedagogical Framework (NCPF) positions children at the centre of all our thinking and actions (Figure S2.1). Rather than presenting any early learning goals or targets, this framework is mindful of the holistic and infinitely connected learning occurring in a child from the moment they are consciously aware. It then asks us to think about the behaviours we facilitate,

DOI: 10.4324/9781003327073-12

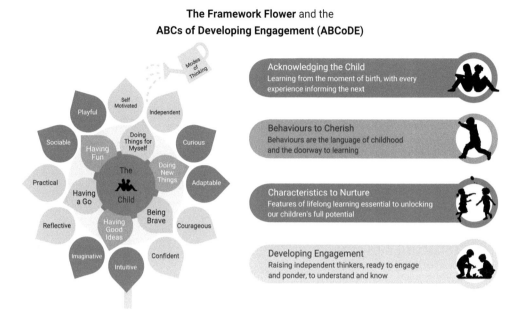

The Framework Flower and the
ABCs of Developing Engagement (ABCoDE)

Figure S2.1: The Nurturing Childhoods Pedagogical Framework Represented by the Framework Flower.

how we encourage them through our actions and the opportunities we give our children to think for themselves. It does this whilst remaining aware of what a child's behaviours are telling us as the characteristics or dispositions underpinning them are developing and allowing these learning process to take root.

As we look to the key features of the framework, let us begin by noting that its beauty comes from its natural simplicity (Figure S2.2). As a pedagogy it runs alongside any statutory curriculum or framework, offering an additional lens through which to understand children's actions and behaviours. Everything is led by the child; no special equipment or environments are required, there are no narrowly defined expectations and there are no boxes to tick. This also means that it is not about to change along with a new government initiative or change of approach. Neither does it matter where in the world you are regulated, or even the year you are reading these words. Nurturing practice is both universal and timeless.

As you begin to look at children through these lenses, you will learn to look beyond the contents of any programme or curriculum. By focusing on helping children to master their naturally evolving dispositions, rather than looking to apply any adult-imposed agenda, you will observe not only deep-felt learning, but also what it means for your children to try to learn. You will recognise their complete concentration as they become absorbed in new experiences. You will see their engagement as their minds and bodies develop at rapid rates. And you will learn to recognise every experience you share as a step on the monumental journey they are on.

KEY FEATURES OF THE

Nurturing Childhoods Framework

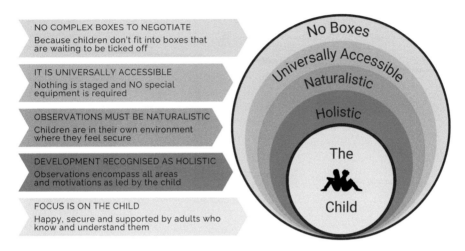

NO COMPLEX BOXES TO NEGOTIATE
Because children don't fit into boxes that
are waiting to be ticked off

IT IS UNIVERSALLY ACCESSIBLE
Nothing is staged and NO special
equipment is required

OBSERVATIONS MUST BE NATURALISTIC
Children are in their own environment
where they feel secure

DEVELOPMENT RECOGNISED AS HOLISTIC
Observations encompass all areas
and motivations as led by the child

FOCUS IS ON THE CHILD
Happy, secure and supported by adults who
know and understand them

No Boxes
Universally Accessible
Naturalistic
Holistic
The Child

Figure S2.2: The Nurturing Childhoods Framework is unique for its central focus on the developing child, rather than any learning goals that serve only to draw focus away.

But more than all of this, it is my hope that you will come to realise the magnitude of every moment we are privileged to spend with young children and the responsibility we have to raise this recognition in the hearts and minds of all the other adults in their lives, whether you are caring for one child or responsible for the development of hundreds of minds throughout an organisation.

The NCPF in practice

Through the following six chapters we will then explore each of these six observable behaviours and the dispositions underpinning them. We finish with a look at the modes of thinking that unite them all. We will look at their importance, how we can develop a child's abilities and desires to explore them and the practices, environments and experiences that facilitate them. We begin during these first years of life, before drawing our attention to the abilities and motivations of older children in subsequent books in this series. But that said, you will also notice a distinct lack of monthly age boundaries or expectations. This framework applies to all learners, regardless of age, and whilst your attention needs to adapt in line with the child in front of you, the framework and its ability to support and nurture our children's development remains constant.

So, as we go through these next chapters, I invite you to think of a young child you know well. If one doesn't easily come to mind, think of yourself as a very young child and embrace this call to arms as we actively help raise this awareness for all our children, firstly here in young babies, then with the additional mobility of our toddlers, the added sense of agency experienced in the years before they transition into school and then through their first experiences of the school classroom as you explore this framework and its additional tools in the other books in this series.

Nurturing Babies to do things for themselves

Doing Things For Myself
BECOMING SELF-MOTIVATED AND INDEPENDENT

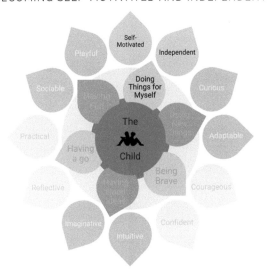

Figure 11.1: Doing Things For Myself - Becoming Self-Motivated and Independent
When we nurture babies opportunities to do things for themselves, they develop the self-motivation and sense of independence that allows them to do it for themselves next time.

In this chapter we focus our attentions on nurturing babies as they do things for themselves, developing the self-motivation and the sense of independence that allows them to do so (Figure 11.1).

To maximise the knowledge and understanding that a child is developing, they need opportunities to do things for themselves. This is such a strong instinct that as soon as all their basic needs are met, they will be driven to pursue it. However, if something regularly gets in the way of this enthusiasm or they are met with obstructions, a child will simply learn not to bother.

DOI: 10.4324/9781003327073-13

For a child to persist with a new skill for the length of time they need to learn and master it, despite the setbacks and frustrations that will be involved, they need to be motivated to do so, as well as have the independence that allows them to try. When these dispositions or tendencies are in place, children will be naturally compelled to explore for themselves. This is a deeply rewarding desire and a young child will soon become frustrated if prevented from it too often.

As children are given opportunities to direct their own explorations, they not only experience the great joy that this brings, but they also gain the skills and freedoms that promote their further success. As they independently explore, they can then rehearse their skills, developing a personal awareness of their body and its needs. As they experience the satisfaction of independently achieving their goals, they are motivated to do more, promoting their desire to continue and embedding persistence even in the absence of external praise or reward.

Knowledge

Know why it is important for babies to do things for themselves

As soon as a child is born they are motivated by the desire to experience everything, reaching out and grasping the things around them. Once they can release those things, new possibilities present themselves as they grasp something new and their independent choice begins to flourish. Soon they will be supporting their head, then their bodies. And once greater mobility is possible, their independent explorations will bring them limitless joyful rewards, the delight of which you will see expressed through every reaction, provided they are permitted to discover them (Figure 11.2).

However, when we find ourselves with a very small child, it can be all too easy to pass them the toy they are reaching for. We might be quick to move them to where they want to go, or find it faster to feed them rather than clean up the mess of them trying to feed themselves. But a child is using these experiences to nurture their growing bodies and developing minds, and every time we do these things for them we are taking this opportunity away. Before long, they learn that their attempts are not worth their efforts and it is easier to motivate someone else to do it for them; their self-motivated desires to reach out and try begin to fade.

If, on the other hand, a child experiences the thrill of making the toy come

Figure 11.2: Every time a child experiences doing something for themselves, the world becomes all the more exciting and worth the efforts of exploring.

towards them by pulling on the blanket or managing their body movements, they begin to develop a sense of their own abilities. Along with this comes the desire to see what else they can do. As their bodies get stronger and their minds more capable, they discover greater possibilities, and the world becomes an increasingly fascinating place to explore their growing independence.

Understanding

Understand how to develop a baby's ability and desire to do things for themselves

As we have learnt, babies are born with all the self-motivation they need to learn, and they are drawn towards the experiences that will help them with this. Even when encouragement and guidance may be lacking, they are keen to explore with all the independence they need. The first thing you need to do is offer a safe environment where they are permitted these new experiences. Then, allow them the freedoms to access them.

When we allow children opportunities to do things for themselves, their natural motivations for learning are validated and encouraged. This may well come with some inflated ideas of what they are capable of, and mistakes will be made. But through these attempts, they're developing an understanding of how their body works, along with a greater understanding of the laws of physics, even the tolerance levels of the dog. But for these benefits to take root, we need to step back and give children the opportunities to try. Otherwise, they will simply stop trying as opportunities to experience the rewards of gaining new skills for themselves are lost.

Firstly, consider the organisation of the day and avoid over-managing their time or routines. For very young children to do things for themselves, they need the time and opportunity to do so unhampered by expectations or routine. An opportunity will take longer to occur to them than it might to older children, and figuring out how to go about it will also take greater time to process. So, for the child who is moved from activity to activity or is frequently whisked away for a poorly timed nappy change, this burgeoning desire is interrupted. So, watch a child before stepping in. When you do need to offer support, do so discreetly so that their focus remains on their chosen fascination rather than becoming drawn to you.

Their abilities are also changing on a daily basis, so adjust the support you offer. Understand their capabilities as you resist the urge to make things too easy or be too quick to jump to their aid. Allow room for independence as you give the help that is required rather than the help that was needed yesterday. And manage the environment so that they can be independent in their movements, placing items where they can move to them or see and indicate their desire for them for themselves.

Support

Be supported in offering practice, environments and experiences where babies can do things for themselves

As a child becomes more stable and then more mobile, their self-motivated interest with their environment will develop. As they gain greater control of their bodies, encourage them to grasp and release objects that they can choose for themselves. As their strength develops and they can support their head, prop them up so they can see the choices available for themselves. Able to sit unaided, even with the support of cushions, they are now able to reach out and select from an array of possibilities around them. And once their bodies strengthen and they gain mobility, whole environments open up to them.

So, mindfully stage an environment where it is safe for children to explore and move around and then allow them to do so. The biggest barrier you will face in supporting babies to do things for themselves is likely to be the well-meaning adults around them. Therefore, your first task is to help those adults understand the importance of allowing children these experiences and then to work to support each other as you mindfully facilitate it.

As you consider the spatial arrangement of the environment, consider placement of furniture that will allow for independent movement. Be mindful of the comfortable space available on the floor and the furniture that allows for cruising. Think about where a water bottle might be positioned or snacks where a child can indicate if they are hungry.

As children begin to independently engage with their environment, you can encourage their explorations by carefully positioning enticing objects and interesting experiences around them. Be mindful of their age and stage of development and ensure these are difficult enough to be interesting, but not too difficult as to lose their interest. Whilst being mindful of creating unnecessary frustrations, offer them slightly greater challenges as they develop their independence and a greater potential sense of reward.

As they start to engage, be mindful of their need for longer thinking time and avoid offering support prematurely. Instead, hold back until it is clear that their struggles are becoming too frustrating to hold any positive benefits. When you jump in too quickly you are denying children this time they need to work something out for themselves (Figure 11.3).

Figure 11.3: When you allow young children the additional time to do something for themselves, their responses may surprise you!.

When children are permitted the joy of discovery, especially once this is motivated by their previous experiences, a child will be compelled to do more. However, their underdeveloped thinking processes also mean that their focus can be easily distracted. So, take care to avoid disrupting their efforts prematurely and allow them to return frequently to tasks that may have been left too soon.

12 Nurturing babies to do new things

Doing New Things
BECOMING CURIOUS AND ADAPTABLE

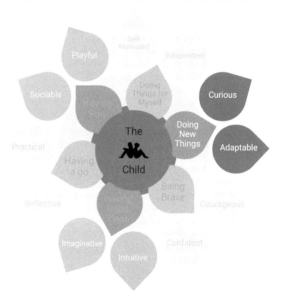

Figure 12.1: Doing New Things - Becoming Curious and Adaptable When we nurture babies opportunities to do new things, they can experience what it means to be curious and adapt to changing circumstances, allowing these dispositions to develop.

In this chapter we are going to focus our attentions on nurturing babies as they do new things, developing the curiosity to want to and the ability to adapt when things change (Figure 12.1).

Children will naturally display an enthusiasm for new opportunities, the more exciting the better. Provided they feel safe and secure within their environment, they are drawn to the novel and this is a great way of encouraging children's desire to do new things. You only need to introduce a new toy into the environment to see this in action, or place an unfamiliar box in the middle of the floor. A child's curiosity – a powerful

DOI: 10.4324/9781003327073-14

learning medium – will then see them eager to investigate and seek out learning opportunities. And as they look to explore these new experiences they are also gaining a constant reward for their efforts that will prompt similar investigations the next time they are presented with a new opportunity.

When children are familiar with new experiences, they become more adaptable to change. Unfazed by a disruption to normal routine, they are able to utilise any learning opportunity, wherever it may arise, without the stress levels that may be experienced by a less adaptable child. If a child has not developed a degree of adaptability, they may quickly become unsettled by anything new, restricting these opportunities for learning and making them less open to exploring new environments, experiencing wide-ranging sensations or hearing the varied languages and tones around them as they build their skills and abilities through their experiences.

Knowledge

Know why it is important for babies to do new things

Children are naturally curious and intensely interested in their world. They are compelled to investigate every object and engage with the people around them as they observe the world and everything in it. When we allow a young child to do new things, we give them an opportunity to explore this curiosity and deepen their understanding of the experience as they retain this enthusiastic sense of exploration. And if we can connect these experiences to their senses, more synapses are triggered, and the experience becomes more deeply rewarding. Children then need opportunities that are mindful of their capabilities and within their reach, mentally and physically. If experiences become too repetitive, these synapses are not stimulated in the same way and their experiences of them soon become unfulfilling and, eventually, not worth pursuing.

Doing new things also speaks of novelty, of keeping things fresh and not following a consistent, regimented plan (Figure 12.2). Whilst babies do need the security of familiar routines and processes, we must take care to avoid becoming too rigid, especially as a child becomes more aware of the world around them. Life does not always run like clockwork, and if it did we would miss out on those marvellous 'in the moment' opportunities that we could not have planned for. When we introduce children to new things from an early age,

Figure 12.2: Change doesn't always mean something huge. Sometimes something as simple as touching a pipe cleaner for the first time can prompt a child's curiosity and encourage a range of new responses.

they are more able to take the unexpected in their stride and embrace possibility without feeling stressed by it. But to foster these responses in your growing children, you need to be open to them too. As you relax into the new and unexpected you can take advantage of all the opportunities around you and avoid your children feeling high levels of stress in adapting and changing situations.

Understanding

Understand how to develop a baby's ability and desire to do new things

Your children will automatically feel an inner need to investigate and explore their environment. And if you do not offer adequate stimulation for them, they will either become quickly frustrated or find stimulation elsewhere – perhaps in ways you may wish they had not. This is a natural instinct and there is little you need to do to prompt this desire. Provided, that is, that the opportunities are there, they are not being pulled away from them and they are not learning from the reluctance of others.

As you offer children a wide range of opportunities that look to encourage and stimulate their natural curiosity, it is important to consider how they are receiving these experiences. If need be, get down to their level to see things from their point of view. Sit or lay on the floor to see how it feels on their knees or their hands. If your children have seemed reluctant to try the new experiences you have offered, consider if this could be the reason.

As their stability develops, provide interesting objects for them to reach for, using their whole bodies as they move towards them to see what they can do. This will bring a range of challenges that a baby is learning to overcome, so manage any that are denying them the chance to explore. Consider whether they can see that something is there. Are they able to reach it? Is the enticement drowned out by all the other sensory stimulation within the room? As their body control improves, so too will your opportunities, but this will also include a greater range of obstacles. So, once risk has been managed, use their mobility and greater understanding to offer a wider range of enticements. Include things that react to the child's touch, perhaps in unexpected ways, things they can find or discover for themselves as their curiosity widens. And repeat experiences for them to revisit from before.

Ensure that your plans for the day can adapt so that you may optimise and capture opportunities as they present themselves. For example, if the child's play is deep and engaging, resist automatically breaking it to follow a scheduled routine. Instead, consider whether a nappy change or bottle can wait until a natural break is reached. As you allow routines and experiences to be flexible to your children's needs, they will learn that it is worth their effort to pursue their curiosities, secure in the knowledge that they will not be taken away just as they were curious enough to try something new.

Support

Be supported in offering practice, environments and experiences where babies can do new things

When we become familiar with caring for children on a regular basis it can become easy to settle into familiar routines. We may come to know the practices that seem to work effectively and find ourselves utilising well-known resources and techniques before we have given them much thought. But whilst we may experience this second week in May many times, this is the only May your child will experience as a baby. The growth and development that is occurring here and now is fleeting, and every opportunity must be taken to make each day interesting and new.

When you offer new and interesting resources that children can freely explore, their natural curiosity will be aroused. When this includes sensory-rich experiences, children will be attracted by the sights, sounds and smells, keen to see what they taste like, how they might feel and what new things they can do with them. Be mindful of this as you offer experiences that are safe for them to explore while offering this level of interest. You might like to include real fruits and vegetables such as corn on the cob with leaves that can be removed, bright yellow against green to look at and bumpy textures to explore, alongside oranges that they can taste as they feel the juices trickle down their arms (Figure 12.3).

Figure 12.3: When we offer children real fruit, they are stimulated through all the senses. You can start with something familiar before moving on to really unusual shapes and textures to arouse their curiosity.

You might like to present resources in different ways; slightly hidden in a treasure basket or under a blanket. Conceal objects in sand or around the environment as you encourage their curious explorations. Play with toys that have unexpected responses or are found in unexpected places. And be sure to keep children's focus by offering things that are exciting and new, that do not always work as expected or fit in the same ways.

When you present activities for children to discover and access for themselves, they will naturally be more curious about them. You can enhance this further by allowing a freedom of choice to direct their interests, rather than presuming what they need or will be interested in. You might also like to offer activities that you are not in control of as you play with older children or spend time with animals. Through these experiences children will hear new language as they develop their vocabularies, they will see different behaviours and explore new things you could not have planned for.

Be aware of everything you could utilise as a learning opportunity; an unexpected trip to the park, local events or sudden windy weather that you must go and feel as a multisensory, whole-body experience. If you can be organised, you can react to these opportunities as they happen, ready to respond to a sudden change. Have special items packed in a bag such as floaty scarves for windy days or umbrellas for when it rains. In these moments children can experience the enjoyment that adapting to unexpected opportunities can bring.

13 Nurturing babies to be brave

Being Brave
BECOMING COURAGEOUS AND CONFIDENT

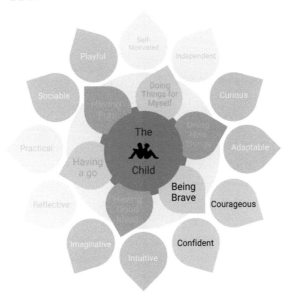

Figure 13.1: Being Brave - Becoming Courageous and Confident When we offer babies opportunities to be brave, they can experience their courage and confidence in ways that permit these dispositions to develop.

In this chapter we are going to focus our attentions on nurturing babies to be brave, developing the courage and confidence to feel a greater sense of security and well-being and developing these dispositions ready to support all the experiences to come (Figure 13.1).

We all need an element of bravery in our lives if we are to grasp the opportunities that present themselves to us and go after the things we want. For a very young child, simply being in a new environment or around unfamiliar faces requires a degree of bravery. But to develop this bravery, children need to experience what it means to try things they are not yet confident in, with the encouragement and support of the trusted adults around them.

DOI: 10.4324/9781003327073-15

By having the courage to try new things and then gaining positive experiences through doing them, children are developing their confidence. It is important that we do not let our own fears or anxieties get in the way of their progress. Children need to take risks, to see what they can do and to understand the skills or abilities that they need to tackle next. As children develop this courage to try new things, they are stretching what they believe to be their limits, and in doing so, are achieving greater rewards that fuel their bravery the next time a new experience presents itself – all of which is a natural part of the learning process. And once experienced, courageous explorations can then follow, provided these have been enjoyable the first time around.

When children are given opportunities to respond to these positive experiences their confidence grows, both within their environment and in their own abilities. This will then fuel their motivations to pursue more advanced learning in new environments and situations, offering the self-assurance and enthusiasm they need to successfully approach the next challenge.

Knowledge

Know why it is important for babies to be brave

To a baby, being brave means many things. It could involve being around new people, experiencing a new environment or a different sensation such as touching paint or feeling the grass between their toes. When they experience these moments of courageous exploration, they are learning what it means to push their limits, while in the safety and security of your care. Through careful selection of the challenges that are offered, you can promote a sense of achievement without undermining this confidence they have in themselves. And once this is in place, they will feel secure enough to seek the challenges that enable them to access new learning experiences.

But they also need to do this without picking up on your fears. Every child goes through phases of only wanting to be held by a certain someone, of being unable to manage when a situation changes or feeling unsure about a new experience. Your responses to them during these moments will inform how well their courage develops, ready to embrace the learning opportunities that will come, as well as developing their levels of confidence in those moments. This will depend strongly on how secure their attachments are with you and how established their general level of well-being is (Figure 13.2).

Figure 13.2: A good attachment with a certain someone gives us the confidence and courage to bravely tackle all the new experiences of the day.

When children are very young, they tend to be naturally and confidently optimistic. Having not yet experienced too many setbacks or failed attempts, they are keen to forge ahead with any experience. While this does take some safeguarding and mindful consideration of environments, we should take care not to diminish their enthusiastic desire to explore and find things out. And yet, when caring for children it can be natural to want to protect them from risk, to manage any possibility of them feeling afraid or coming to harm. However, children need to learn what it means to push their limits, to see where these are and to experience the thrill of extending them.

Understanding

Understand how to develop a baby's ability and desire to be brave

When it comes to social situations, very young children can struggle, especially when finding themselves in a strange environment or surrounded with unfamiliar people. But finding a level of courage and confidence in all these situations is a core part of safeguarding a child's mental well-being within them. There will be times when a child needs to face the unfamiliar and we want our children to feel comfortable in their uncertainty. This will take maturity to understand that loved ones do come back or that a hungry tummy will not last forever, but in the meantime, there is a lot we can do to support their courageous outlook.

The first step is to ensure your children are well attached to the key people in their life. This is rooted in the personal experiences you share together and the acts of kindness that identify you as someone to be trusted and relied upon. Secondly, ensure they are comfortable in their surroundings. We know that children respond through their senses, but too much stimulation can be overwhelming, so look to achieve a calming balance. Then, with a secure knowledge of your children's abilities, include a variety of tasks for them to freely select in their play, designed to gently stretch these abilities. Allow them the freedom to explore their environment and its resources at their own pace, with independent choices they can make as they tentatively try the things they feel ready and sufficiently confident for. As their courage grows, they will learn the pleasure of challenging their existing physical and cognitive boundaries, becoming braver with each new experience.

Try to encourage free physical exploration, avoiding confining their movements to bouncy chairs or segregated areas. Alongside this, offer activities that will naturally bolster their confidence as they experience the things they can do. You can also develop their confidence through repetition with familiar patterns in a favoured book or predictable experiences within routines, paired with opportunities to trial their own ideas and investigations. As a belief in their own capabilities is reinforced, their confidence in new tasks will grow along with the self-esteem that develops through them. With profound effects on their emotional well-being, this sense of personal gratification that is developing will encourage bravery for the next challenge that must be faced.

Support

Be supported in offering practice, environments and experiences where babies can be brave

If we are to offer practice, environments and experiences where babies can be brave, we must firstly be brave ourselves. This may mean stepping outside of our own comfort zones, trialling new things or having a greater faith in the abilities of our young children. While it may be tempting to wrap children in cotton wool, this is doing them a gross disservice. Whilst limiting the opportunities and experiences you need to be offering them, they will also pick up on your fears and anxieties, potentially making them fearful of the very things that will stimulate great personal growth and understanding.

Your children will be developing in mind and body every day. Alongside their increased mobility is their impulse to move and explore their environment, to engage with the people in it and to see what they themselves are capable of. You can encourage this by allowing your children the freedoms they need as they explore their developing sense of courageous bravery. Make sure they feel protected and secure through your reassuring tones and interactions; at the same time, where you can, resist assisting too early or limiting their direction of enquiry.

Offer challenges that stretch their abilities, as they reach out for objects. Games such as peekaboo, hiding objects under blankets or books with flaps introduce the pleasure of discovery as they build the courage to try something new (Figure 13.3). Rather than automatically preventing them from approaching the climbing wall, consider what your new crawler might actually do when they get there. Are they likely to climb to great heights and fall off, or simply explore a new area? At the same time, be aware of excessive frustrations when something is too developmentally advanced for them. To help manage this you might like to offer a range of activities that they can choose from, with those they can succeed at with ease, until they feel more courageous, increasing in complexity as their confidence grows.

Figure 13.3: Games of peekaboo can be hugely thrilling as babies take the risk of losing you from sight, developing their sense of bravery with every repetition.

Through the day, look to recognise a child's need to pacify themselves as they contemplate more difficult tasks. This may involve the need of a comforter or a toy to mouth as they consider how to grasp the car and make it move. Their confidence levels are also likely to change throughout the day as they become tired, so ensure alternative options are offered that are just as rewarding, perhaps with different options that vary the task, allowing them to persist rather than you needing to complete the task for them.

14 Nurturing babies to have good ideas

Having Good Ideas

BECOMING INTUITIVE AND IMAGINATIVE

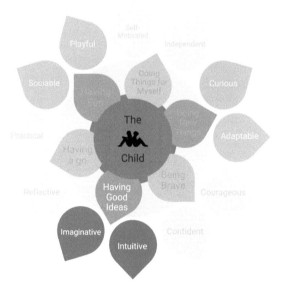

Figure 14.1: Having Good Ideas - Becoming Intuitive and Imaginative When we allow babies opportunities to have their own ideas, they experience what it means to be intuitive and to use their imagination, encouraging these dispositions to develop.

In this chapter we are going to focus our attentions on nurturing babies as they have good ideas, using their intuition and imagination as they develop these powerful tools of learning (Figure 14.1).

Nurturing a young baby's abilities as they demonstrate the ideas they are having may seem like an odd thing to think about. But gaze into the eyes of a very young child and you will see a great deal of activity occurring. Children are being bombarded with information from around their environment every second of every day, along with the

DOI: 10.4324/9781003327073-16

interactions they are having with everyone in it. As their developing mind absorbs all of this information, it needs to try to sort it all out. To do so, it will explore what it thinks to be the case. When this is correct, intuition kicks in to affirm this knowledge. And when something is not quite right, corrections and adaptations can be made.

But for all of this to happen, a child must trial the ideas they are having, learning as they hypothesise about how their hand moves through the air, why they hear a sound when an object falls or the effect their smile has on another person. By testing and reaffirming their ideas through every experience they gain, their imagination is fuelling the learning processes that they are looking to develop. And when they are permitted the opportunities to follow their intuitive responses, their confidence in these processes and their motivation to follow their instincts flourish, enabling children to seek out and access their own learning opportunities, drawing logical conclusions from them as they make the necessary links. But all of these ideas need opportunities to try as we develop a child's active imagination and allow them to explore their inspiration and intuitive reactions.

Knowledge

Know why it is important for babies to have good ideas

When you see a child have an idea and put it in action, you are seeing evidence of their imagination and their intuition in that moment (Figure 14.2). This will look and feel somewhat different for a tiny baby than it will for a toddler or an older child and yet their brain is no less active. While an older child may plan an elaborate project, a baby will be looking at the bricks around them and considering whether to hit them together, to put them in their mouths or push them aside and practice crawling again. As children process the rich information from all around them, they are learning what they can do with it. And as they do so, they are experiencing the power of turning observation and imagination into action. Provided they are permitted to do so, they are also experiencing what this potential can mean.

Figure 14.2: Do I move it, hit it, throw it... or go for a snack? What can I imagine doing next and what does my developing intuition tell me will happen if I do?

Patterns of intuitive behaviour can be seen in a child from the time they are born, as they turn towards milk or use the power of a smile to engage others in emotional reactions. But to extend and strengthen this powerful skill of simply knowing something requires a bank of diverse and relatable experiences that they are ready to employ.

Every time a baby is presented with new resources to manipulate, to touch and to mouth, they are being given another opportunity to advance this growing imagination. Developing processes that began as instinct, a child will be drawn to these new encounters as they enhance their bank of experiences. They will be considering what this opportunity will be like and making decisions around whether they wish to have it, what they might do with it and how this relates to experiences they have had in the past. All of this supports their enhancing levels of intuition as their imagination develops.

Understanding

Understand how to develop a baby's ability and desire to have good ideas

In the very early days it may seem like young children are not doing much theorising. They may not seem to be using their imagination or intuition to think of ideas for themselves. But you would be surprised. As a child watches everything around them, they are taking it all in. You can support this process by letting very young children watch the interactions and play of older children as they freely demonstrate their ideas and behaviours. Before long you will see a much younger child trying similar techniques for themselves.

It is then so important that we take care not to make assumptions about what a child is thinking and that we avoid judging their early attempts as insignificant or stunt their endeavours by denying them access to the opportunities they need to try. It is also important that we remember a very young child's thinking processes are on a different timescale to our own. They need a longer time to process their ideas and to consider what they want to do next, so avoid clearing these opportunities away too quickly. You might like to offer familiar experiences to trigger their memories as they imagine what might come next, all the while ensuring that their intuitive behaviours are not overlooked, disapproved of or devalued.

Give them the time and opportunity they need to follow their natural instincts, without being too quick to "entertain" or steer them in a different direction. Provided these experiences are designed for their rich source of information, they will provide valuable information that a child can later build upon. Allow children to follow their natural intuitions as they grasp and mouth objects. They will want to do this with everything, so before you limit this intuitive response by perhaps taking the paints away, think about how you can adapt their experiences so that this powerful learning experience can be utilised. Possibly try replacing traditional paints with brightly coloured yoghurt or fruit purees. If splashing in the water tray is making too much mess inside, take the play outdoors. By remembering your goal here is to maximise the learning opportunities rather than create a finished product, you can allow children to make deeper connections in their learning and gain the experiences to inform their intuitive instincts for next time.

Support

Be supported in offering practice, environments and experiences where babies can have good ideas

As your children explore their environment and the opportunities you offer them within it, let them do so in their own ways. Avoid having too many firm ideas of your own ahead of time and instead, follow their lead as you let them experience their own ideas and ways of doing things (Figure 14.3). Children are not limited by the conventions that we can find ourselves unthinkingly falling into. When we resist assuming a conventional use of an object or conforming to expected outcomes in front of children, they are able to explore resources and their many uses in their own way. When

Figure 14.3: The human brain loves pattern and repetition and a child will intuitively be expecting it. You can see this in action when you use repeating patterns as you clap or make something unexpected happen.

we offer them a tea set to play with, they are not confined by tea drinking role play and provided we avoid directing the play in this way, they can use the items to explore a range of ideas, such as trialling cause and effect as objects bang into one another, or causing a reaction with one from their actions on another. They may investigate schema by transporting the items, rolling them or hiding them all under blankets.

As children are permitted to follow their own thoughts and insights, remember that at this age this will undoubtedly incorporate trialling every new idea with their mouth. Full of sensory receptors, the mouth is a vital source of information that a child will intuitively utilise to inform their enquiries. So, offer resources that they can safely explore in this way. This may include toys that are designed with this purpose in mind, but also fruits and vegetables, wooden spoons and metal cups. As you utilise their senses as a way of stimulating their imagination, children can explore their understanding of the properties of these items through a range of materials and textures. They may explore their ideas about how the shiny items may feel, exploring how some feel cold, while others are warm. Having put something rough on their tongue, they may try an alternative as they utilise their imagination to consider the outcome.

As children explore their ideas they will also be relying on their intuition about what they can do and how they should go about it. You can develop their intuition by hiding items that you then find together, repeating the game by concealing things back in the same places. Play clapping games that use repeating patterns or involve a change after every third clap as you introduce a dramatic reaction that they learn to respond to.

When you then offer experiences that are similar to familiar ones, a child can apply their previous experiences to the things they have been given today. When this becomes a common practice that they learn to rely on, their initial responses may become instinctive as they seem to know a range of possibilities intuitively, building a greater repertoire of new ideas with every response.

15 Nurturing babies to have a go

Having a Go
BECOMING REFLECTIVE AND PRACTICAL

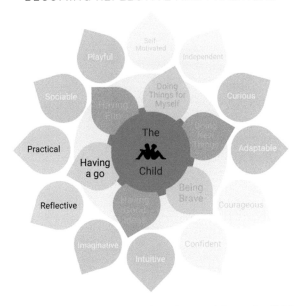

Figure 15.1: Having a Go – Becoming Reflective and Practical When babies are given opportunities to have a go for themselves, they can develop practical skills and gain the experiences they will reflect upon, nurturing these dispositions as they develop.

In this chapter we are going to focus our attentions on nurturing babies as they develop the abilities and desires to have a go, developing the practical skills that allow them to do so and the deeply impactful opportunities to reflect that follow (Figure 15.1).

When children have opportunities to have a go with things for themselves, they experience the learning opportunities on offer throughout their entire body rather than simply letting someone else do it while they look on. In doing so they are gaining practical experiences that develop a range of skills throughout the body, strengthening fine

DOI: 10.4324/9781003327073-17

and gross motor development as well as their manual dexterity and the deep-rooted connections within their cognitive understanding.

These experiences will also encourage their confidence to embrace future practical learning opportunities, allowing further skills to be enhanced. They will have informed children's understanding of how objects work, as well as how they react with one another, the forces the child needs to apply to make something happen, the impact when they do and how to manage their own body as they take on the task without toppling over.

When you then pair these experiences with opportunities to reflect on what has been done, the knowledge is absorbed and assimilated, developing reflective skills that allow children to consider alternative methods of achieving a task even before they are aware of the process. When this is in place, children are more inclined to persevere rather than give up after a first attempt as they become informed by the alternative approaches they have trialled and observed.

Knowledge

Know why it is important for babies to have a go

As we know, children are continuously learning through all the experiences they are permitted to have. This primarily happens through their senses and their movements as they gain the knowledge they need to inform their learning. Access to ongoing practical experiences takes this learning to another level as they combine their mental and physical learning to develop a greater sense of their own abilities (Figure 15.2). But learning is not a spectator sport and children need to have a go at it. They know this before many unsuspecting adults tend to as anything within their reach becomes fair game, from the hair that needs to be pulled to the potted plant that needs to be tipped over.

Practical opportunities to play and experience how something feels, tastes or moves informs your young learner about how their world operates while at the same time equipping them with the tools they need to approach all the new situations that are yet to come. All this too enticing to resist; however, a child

Figure 15.2: When experiencing practical activities, children learn through their whole body.

also needs opportunities to consider and internalise what they have learnt from before.

Having observed others at play or having experienced new activities for themselves, a baby then needs opportunities to reflect on these experiences as their memories are processed and sorted out. You will recognise these moments in their frequent need for sleep and "down time", after which they will be keen to experiment again, trying and adapting their approach as they strive to achieve what they could not before. Or they'll go back a second time just to check they have things right, no matter how many times they have been asked to leave the plant alone. These hands-on experiences are then of foundational importance to all the deep and complex learning that is to come, and it is important that we offer our children a diverse and accessible range of them.

Understanding

Understand how to develop a baby's ability and desire to have a go

Offered a range of interesting items that they can engage with, children will feel compelled to have a go for themselves. However, sometimes they may initially seem reluctant and will need a moment, perhaps even opportunities to see other children playing and engaging within a range of tasks. Again, they may need a little additional time as they consider what they have seen and internalise what this means for themselves, reflecting on what they have been observing around them before being ready to have a go themselves.

To encourage their participation, their abilities and stage of development need to be considered, especially if they are in a new environment or are less than familiar with the people in it. This then requires opportunities that have been practically considered and thought through, within an accessible environment that they feel both safe and secure in. You can offer children a greater sense of protection and ease by adding elements of familiarity around them and letting them proceed at their own pace.

If you provide lots of familiar resources, a child can begin to make practical assumptions based on their previous experiences. As they then trial and explore the additional items you add, perhaps with different responses and outcomes, their interest can be further stimulated – especially when some reactions are unexpected or need some working out. For example, if certain items will fit in a container while others will not, or if some fabrics crinkle while others feel soft and fluffy. You can also introduce new elements into their play with similar properties and new possibilities as their understanding develops, for example extending simple sand play to include areas that have been moistened.

Children's understanding needs lots of repetition and repeat visits as they use, test and challenge their evolving knowledge of a concept. At this age, their focus will mainly be on the present, so repeated experiences need to be provided fairly quickly if they are to make meaning from them. You can then extend these opportunities by allowing children to effect practical change, such as splashing in water, moving things, grasping objects or causing sound and light effects. Over time, these authentic, practical experiences allow children to make sense of what is happening, essential for the more complex ideas that will follow. As they internally reflect, their learning is strengthened, making further connections in their learning with every opportunity they have to revisit.

Support

Be supported in offering practice, environments and experiences where babies can have a go

When you engage with very young children, aim to include different practical experiences in your play. As they look to reach out and grasp things for themselves, be mindful of these instincts and ensure the objects they want to grasp are safe for them to do so. Let them see what you are doing, for example stirring something in a bowl, and then allow them to have a go for themselves. You may then like to leave the items available for them to try, perhaps moving away while they think things through before coming back to have a go when they are ready. Allow the time it takes for a child to ponder their actions and consider their observations, reflecting on what they have seen while you resist giving cues or prematurely directing their actions (Figure 15.3).

Figure 15.3: Sometimes we may need a moment to think about what we want to do or whether we want to do it. Having the resources available for when we are ready allows for this to happen.

You may then like to include authentic items and play resources. By including things that are the same or similar to items they see being used, they can explore the practical skills they have watched being demonstrated for themselves, for example hairbrushes, toothbrushes, paintbrushes and cleaning brushes. They will then begin to make connections between the places they have seen these items and the repetitive motions embraced in their use. As they trial these techniques for themselves they are internalising practical methods of learning throughout their whole body.

As you offer children opportunities to develop their practical skills, look to include trial and improvement techniques, such as making objects move or to produce a sound. Let them play at fitting objects inside one another, pulling clothes off of a doll or the cause and effect of splashing, pushing or rolling. As you play with them, you may like to show them how to operate different toys in different ways, then leave the items to try for themselves later.

When you do offer things for them to try for themselves, avoid being too quick to change the experiences. Instead, allow children the chance to return, building on their confidence with every visit as their knowledge and understanding grows. When they explore the practical possibilities of the objects at hand they will need to ponder what this means, possibly using them in a different environment or in alternative ways as they try for a while before coming back for a second visit. As they develop their own reflective techniques, offer lots of opportunities to watch other children playing with similar activities. When they then come back to trial the ideas they have seen demonstrated themselves, their learning is being reinforced through multiple angles, especially when you can offer them the same resources to play with.

16 Nurturing babies to have fun

Having Fun
BECOMING PLAYFUL AND SOCIABLE

Figure 16.1: Having Fun - Becoming Playful and Sociable When we offer babies opportunities to have fun, they can enjoy the playful and social experiences that having fun means, encouraging these dispositions as they develop.

In this chapter we are going to focus our attentions on nurturing babies as they have fun, developing the playful experiences and social encounters that encourage these dispositions to develop (Figure 16.1).

Play offers children a safe environment in which to experience and rehearse every idea and concept they need to master. No matter how complex these ideas may currently be to them, they can be embraced with excitement and joy when done in an environment of play and social learning while at the same time stimulating development

DOI: 10.4324/9781003327073-18

across their whole body as they strengthen all systems through their desires to play and have fun.

We are all social beings at heart, hardwired to respond to the eye contact and smiles that a child is hardwired to offer from the first moments of life. Through the warm, positive interactions that you share, a child's language skills flourish. At the same time they are observing and developing the social skills required to engage with others and explore their world.

These social experiences are both rewarding and exciting as they stimulate learning on every level. Once we are fully aware of their potential, we can utilise this to open a child's mind to the rich environment they are in and the endless opportunities within it, all the while laying the foundations for more advanced learning as the skills required are explored and practiced.

Knowledge

Know why it is important for babies to have fun

Children are driven to be playful and sociable; it is how we bond and learn in an environment of collaborative knowledge and understanding that is so important to our species that we are compelled to do it. On a fundamental level, we are all social beings. Keen to engage and have fun in any way that we can, this starts from the first moments of life. From a child's first attempts at making eye contact, a newborn is eager to engage with everyone around them, seeking to make social connections and to start the process of bonding.

Your children have been born into a highly sociable world, ready and able to utilise all their natural abilities to motivate the companionship and attention of others. They will be watching those around them, observing as others interact and learning how these social exchanges work. They will note the behaviours and emotions on display as they rehearse their own use of language, facial expressions and gestures. Using these past experiences and their observations of others, your children will be using play to trial their ideas and actions within safe environments.

Being playful and having fun together allows children to draw companionship and protection towards them. It allows them to approach new situations in unthreatening and safe ways and offers them enjoyable ways of trialling new ideas and learning from the reactions they can entice from those around them. Having fun through playful and social interactions allows children to experience the complex interplays taking place in the world around them. Accessed at their own pace and driven by their own needs, it offers complete emersion in what is the most satisfying of learning experiences whilst at the same time learning the complex social skills that will be important to every future relationship.

Understanding

Understand how to develop a baby's ability and desire to have fun

It might seem strange to suggest that we need to think about encouraging a child to have fun. Their playful and social impulses are a natural instinct; however, they are also easily interrupted. We need to be mindful of this; for example, it is important for babies to wallow in play, so we need to avoid breaking this essential practice by scheduling in nappy changes and snacks. Instead, take care of these and then settle down to play that children can engage in for as long as they want, while you wait for them to indicate that they have naturally had enough.

A very young child will try to engage with you from day one. It is important that you respond to their facial expressions and gestures in all their rudimentary forms. Encourage their emerging two-way communication as it incorporates their face, their hands and whole-body movements. Games that involve you mirroring their movements can offer endless joy. Children also benefit hugely from observing and interacting with older children. So, allow your children to watch others playing and engaging as they learn what it means to participate with older minds, motivating the richly rewarding companionship that these social exchanges bring (Figure 16.2).

Figure 16.2: Through playful, social experiences children are learning new ideas, experiencing different reactions and practicing the complex interplays needed to take their place in this fascinating world.

Where possible you might also like to offer resources to younger children that are similar to those they see their older companions using. The younger children will of course find different uses for these resources initially that are no less fun or engaging for them, so be mindful of the age appropriateness and the uses that may come to mind.

Children also need continual opportunities to access play, so avoid excessive time constrained in a chair or the use of attention-sapping screens or distractions. A young child will also become easily distressed when their responses are blocked or not recognised, so notice and sensitively manage all of their attempts at social engagement with you. Through their social engagements and play children are learning to communicate, but to do so they need to be able to hear both their own voices and those around them, so keep background noise such as continually playing music at a minimum. As you consider their opportunities to engage, especially for less mobile children, consider what is in their line of sight and their access to different environments and opportunities.

Support

Be supported in offering practice, environments and experiences where this can be explored

Children need little encouragement to play and have fun. But they do need environments that allow them to do it in safety with adults who value and support its importance. When you look to offer the most important learning mechanism to your children, consider the time frames in which you are offering it, the environments in which it is staged and how much it is valued by the adults that manage it.

Playful, social experiences benefit from a range of interesting resources, both familiar and new. However, with every new resource you introduce comes a degree of distraction. So, consider the array of sensory stimulation on offer and consider their use. Can a child investigate their ideas about how these may feel? Can they observe how something might react or the possibilities permitted when items are combined? Can they touch, taste and manipulate? Are these items and the "noise" they create worth their while?

Any items you do introduce should be considered for safety so that they can be freely played with. There should be sufficient resources so that sharing, a concept they are far from being ready for, does not become an issue. And you should carefully consider how children learn and combine their experiences, with particular attention to their access to the environment, mindful of their current stage of development.

When this play is then taken outside, a greater level of free exploration is possible. Within the extended opportunities that are permitted outdoors, natural resources might be added in more realistic ways, such as feeling wet sand between their toes, looking at a range of stones or pebbles to select the one they want or the effects of water changing the appearance of the surface it is poured upon. So, take their play outside as often as possible for increased stimulation and freedom (Figure 16.3).

Figure 16.3: So many additional fun possibilities are added simply by taking play outside.

As you think about their environment, consider the play opportunities within every area children spend time in. What can they play with while you change their nappy? What can you give them to explore while you prepare food? How can they direct their enquiries along their own playful directions? Is their two-way babble promoted and encouraged or essentially prevented by excessive background noise, screens or overly distracting environments?

Social interactions are of great importance to these processes. So, be sure to offer your children opportunities to move freely towards social encounters in their play. Avoid segregating children according to their age or securing them in chairs for prolonged periods of time. Instead, provide opportunities for children to play alongside others, watching and participating within different social groupings. Model warm, positive social interactions within stimulating environments that respond to their reactions and attempts. And as you sit with them, provide a point of reference to the children's investigations as you draw them towards you.

17 Nurturing babies to think

The Framework Flower

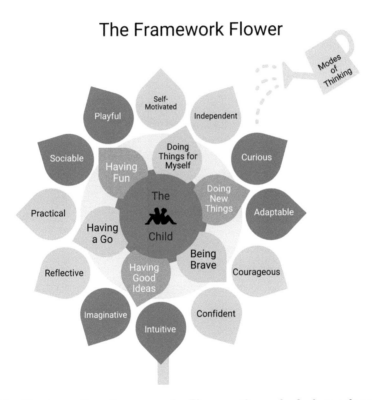

Figure 17.1: Nurture the Framework Flower through Independent Thought
Throughout all our interactions, provocations and permissions, we need to remember that we are raising independent thinkers, ready to engage and ponder, to understand and know.

As we draw this book to a close let us revisit the Framework Flower and draw our attention to the magic that allows all of this dispositional development to really take root … and that is providing our children with the autonomy and permissions to experience what it means to think. To be creative, to simultaneously use different ideas and make connections in their leaning, to think of the bigger picture and take logical leaps (Figure 17.1).

DOI: 10.4324/9781003327073-19

Children are absorbing and contemplating their environment from the moment they enter into it. They are taking in nuggets of information through all their senses and simultaneously combining and processing them as they make sense of the world around them. When you permit these opportunities, their banks of experiences are developed in deeper ways than any discrete experience would permit (Figure 17.2).

Figure 17.2: From the moment a child is born they are taking in their surroundings and processing all the information available to them. These experiences, and what they are permitted to do with them, are then laying the blueprint for how they will think about every future experience.

The opportunities you offer to children to explore their thoughts in various ways are key to this process. By being able to simultaneously combine all areas of learning, children are making connections in their learning. By applying logic and repeated practice to these experiences, children are underpinning their thoughts with evidence to reinforce or challenge their understanding, all the while establishing their foundations for more complex ideas.

As their learning becomes more complex children need strategies to make sense of it. Establishing a repertoire of past experiences prepares them for this. Having experienced the rewards of approaching new challenges in a range of ways, children are more open minded towards learning opportunities. This begins with schematic behaviours that utilise wider ways of thinking and broader approaches before the finer detail of future learning can be fully understood. You can support all of a child's thinking processes by encouraging experiences that are embedded in meaningful contexts. Through these wider opportunities for learning, children become surrounded in opportunities as their developing skills are given meaning.

Knowledge

Know why it is important for babies to think

From the time they are born children have a natural instinct to gather information from the range of different sources they have available to them. Using their eyes and ears simultaneously as they take in their surroundings, along with their hands and mouths to bring their surroundings closer to them, they are thinking deeply about what all of this means, driven to understand as much as they can. They are picking up on and learning to rely on predictable patterns as they develop a sense of rhythm within everyday events. And as they combine their increasing mobility with their instinct for exploration and natural desire to investigate, they show an increased interest in their wider surroundings.

The experiences children are gaining now are also paving the way for the more enhanced methods of thinking and understanding that they will later rely on. Taking in information from various sources and simultaneously processing it is a necessary component of understanding more complex situations and ideas. But what's more, they are also learning about their power to acquire knowledge from different sources and by experiencing new situations. With the knowledge that something can be approached in diverse and creative ways, a child is less confined by expectations, perceived or otherwise.

From the beginning, your role within a child's thought processes is to introduce them to their potential. Through the experiences and play resources you offer, you are guiding and supporting their investigations while allowing them to gain a sense of their own creative thought processes. When permitted these opportunities, they can take in information from many different sources, learning to utilise all their senses as they make deeply powerful connections in their learning. Once familiar with the rewards this can bring, children can become more open minded towards learning opportunities and the approaches that work for them. It is through establishing these patterns that a child can begin to find familiarity within new challenges they face.

Understanding

Understand how to develop a baby's ability and desire to think

When you provide opportunities for a young child to explore and engage with the opportunities you offer to them, their mind will be naturally processing the information it receives. You can encourage this further by making these engagements interesting to them and by avoiding overstimulation. You might like to engage more than one sense at a time, combining objects that are interesting to look at, fabrics of different textures or toys that move in different ways or make unusual noises. You can consider the smells that are surrounding them or the surfaces that they are playing on while avoiding any stimulus that demands all their attention for any period of time, such as a screen.

You can support children's creative ideas by giving them experiences that they can try for themselves, while being mindful of any limits you may be unintentionally imposing. The ideas a young child is trying out may be somewhat different to what you had expected. But given the opportunities to see their ideas in action will stimulate their powerful curiosity. So, support and encourage their explorations as you resist the urge to direct. And let them be creative as they manipulate the things you offer them to explore.

As children strive to make sense of their world, they will seek out every chance to find the patterns within it. They will value opportunities to gaze at the shape of your face, they will take joy in your repeated patterns of behaviour, such as a rhythm you clap out or the repeated actions of you popping out from behind a scarf. As you recognise the important processes occurring behind these simple actions, you can look to offer experiences of predictable logic within your daily routines and lots of fun opportunities for children to try.

When a child's stability allows them to sit up and gaze around the room, they have more opportunity to combine a greater range of information. As their independent movements allow them to reach and grasp, their ideas can be actioned. And as their mobility increases they have greater freedoms to explore their ideas. So, manage any risks that may be limiting their independent and instantaneous thought and allow children the uninterrupted time and access they need to freely explore their thoughts in the moment. As you maximise their access to wide ranges of experiences, you will be increasing their learning opportunities and the wide range of connections they can make.

Support

Be supported in offering practice, environments and experiences where babies can think

As you look to stimulate a child's simultaneous thinking, allow children to access a range of environments. As they explore objects and move them between areas they are freely combining their thinking in different ways. You can add to this synchronised approach by offering multisensory play. Let them enjoy taking off their socks as they feel the grass between their toes while you play at tracking down a repeating insect noise or a fragrant smell. You can also play with relationships between objects as they investigate their understanding of property by exploring with their hands, feet and mouth.

Extend their play to incorporate the dimensions of the space around you; talk about things being under, over, inside or behind as you find the treasures you have hidden in these places. Offer a wide range of resources and let children explore without any predetermined expectations or directions. As they do so, notice the patterns they are noticing. Are they collecting together all the balls? Is it all the little items or the ones that feel nice to the touch? Follow the children's lead as they investigate, being careful not to let your adult knowledge direct them away from their creative thoughts (Figure 17.3).

As you watch their play inside and out you can consider resources that might add a different dimension. If they are fascinated by the water tray, could you set up a puddle outside that they could explore with their whole body? What natural resources could you add to it for different responses? What effect would oil on the surface make as the sunlight hits it? What might they think about seeing some items sink (sand) while others seem to disappear (sprinkled sugar)? You might like to introduce resources that behave in similar ways to each other, such as many different balls that roll when pushed in the same way. Or one that does not behave, weighted to roll in an unexpected path.

It is important that children can keep returning to the same experiences and resources so they can trial their logical ideas about what is happening. Within stimulating environments, you can then show children different opportunities as you play together, then leave them for them to find again. You can also look to include some logical aspects as they investigate, such as the effects of a splash in the water play. Others may involve a change, such as a new colour or some different items that have been added for renewed interest. Through these adaptations you can encourage their increased exploration with new and previously enjoyed resources found in a variety of places.

Figure 17.3: Promote children's thinking by offering similar resources in a variety of ways, in various locations or for unusual purposes as they explore unusual ways of thinking about things.

Index

Pages in *italics* refer to figures.